ADVERTISING

WITHOUT AN AGENCY

A Comprehensive Guide to
Radio, Television, Print, Direct Mail,
and Outdoor Advertising
for Small Business

KATHY J. KOBLISKI

OASIS PRESS BOOKS& SOFTWARE

The Oasis Press®
Central Point, Oregon

Published by The Oasis Press®/PSI Research

© 1998 by Kathy J. Kobliski

This publication is designed to provide accurate and authoritative information in regard to the subject matter covered. It is sold with the understanding that the author and publisher are not engaged in rendering legal, accounting, or other professional service. If legal advice or other expert assistance is required, the services of a competent professional person should be sought.

> *— from a declaration of principles jointly adopted by a committee of the American Bar Association and a committee of publishers.*

Editor: Camille Akin
Interior design: Karen Billipp, Eliot House Productions
Cover illustration and design: Steven Burns
Author portrait: Photography by Jules

Please direct any comments, questions, or suggestions regarding this book to:

The Oasis Press®/PSI Research
Editorial Department
P.O. Box 3727
Central Point, OR 97502-0032

(541) 479-9464
(541) 476-1479 *fax*
info@psi-research.com *e-mail*

The Oasis Press® is a Registered Trademark of Publishing Services, Inc., an Oregon corporation doing business as PSI Research.

Library of Congress Cataloging-in-Publication Data

Kobliski. Kathy J., 1946–
    Advertising without an agency : a comprehensive guide to radio, television, print, direct mail, and outdoor advertising for small business / Kathy J. Kobliski. -- 1st ed.
       p.   cm.
    ISBN 1-55571-429-3
    1. Advertising. 2. Small business.
    HF5823.K624   1998
    659.1--dc21   98-19013
                                                                                                 CIP

Printed and bound in the United States of America

First Edition 10 9 8 7 6 5 4 3 2 1 0

Endorsments

"*Advertising Without an Agency* is an excellent primer for every small business owner to set his/her own marketing program or become a better buyer of media and services. It should be on the 'must read' list of every entrepreneur. . . . Small business owners will improve their bottom line by reading *Advertising Without an Agency*. . . .Kathy Kobliski has combined experience and talent to create a hands-on approach to getting the most from small business advertising."
— Jim King, New York State Director
Albany, New York

"Teaches you in a few hours what would take years to learn on your own. . . . Reading this book will prevent small business owners from making mistakes and learning the hard way. . . . Great tutorial for the beginning or budding entrepreneur."
— Jo Alice Mospan, Small Business Administration District Director
Helena, Montana

"*Advertising Without an Agency* is a thorough reference guide for the perceptive, cost conscious, modern entrepreneur. . . . Taking charge of this vital area, with the help of this book, will improve the quality of public notices while stretching the small businessperson's advertising dollar."
— Robert Andrews, Small Business Administration District Director
St. Louis, Missouri

"Excellent resource for both the start-up business person as well as the existing. . . . Time is money! Take the time to learn from this resource and save yourself a lot of money!"
— Wilfredo Gonzalez, Small Business Administration District Director
Jacksonville, Florida

Dedication

To my family.

Now I can go back to meddling in *your* business.

Contents

Preface

Advertising is not a perfect science. It's not even close. It can be frustrating, confusing, expensive, sometimes overwhelming, and too time consuming for the small business owner who has so many other responsibilities. Thousands of dollars can easily be wasted by making uninformed advertising decisions.

As a small business owner, your budget may not be large enough to interest an advertising agency, so you are left to the mercy of media sales reps who appear daily at your business door. There may be no other facet of your business in which you can be more easily led astray by so many friendly people. The problem is, which ones do you believe? How do you know which radio and television stations are the best ones to use? Which publications and billboards will increase the demand for your product or service?

This book was designed to help you avoid common mistakes and provide time-saving, energy-saving, money-saving information. It is not for the advertising expert who can chew up and spit out information from Arbitron and Nielsen over breakfast. It is for the direct advertiser who must keep up with frequently changing formats and audiences of radio stations, shifting television lineups, special sections of various publications, as well as the stories and "numbers" recited by media sales people — all while trying to meet the many other daily demands of running your business.

Radio is the "Theater of the Mind," but isn't it fleeting? Will anyone be listening to the station your ad is on for that particular :30 or :60 second slot?

Television provides both audio and visual. But doesn't it limit you creatively to the size of your television screen? With all the cable channels and fast forwarding through commercials, how much of your message actually gets through?

Outdoor Advertising is out there from dawn to dusk. But doesn't that limit you to the same travelers day in and day out?

Print is there for you to re-read, circle, and clip out. But is circulation going down? Who has the time to read the paper from cover to cover these days? How many people will actually read the page your ad is on?

Direct Mail can blanket entire or specific communities. But do people read flyers and inserts or do they think of them as "junk mail"?

Yellow Page advertising lends credibility to your business. But do you really want to be jammed on a page with all of your competitors? Do you want your expensive ad leading consumers to your competitors who not only share the page but may have a larger ad?

Now that your advertising anxieties have been raised to a new level, let's take a look at this business from the inside. I hope this book succeeds in taking some of the mystery out of the advertising process, arms you with material to remove much of the guesswork and frustration you may have experienced in the past and allows you to work those advertising dollars harder than ever to grow your business.

Remember that advertising's only job is to make that phone ring, increase traffic in your store, and generate interest in your product or service. Once that response has been achieved it's up to you to come through with friendly, helpful, knowledgeable employees, effective follow through on sales or new clients, and all of the other aspects that go into maintaining consumer or client interest that your advertising has generated.

Advertising takes a lot of time and costs a lot of money. There are many ways to let people know you're open for business. Whether you start by putting flyers on windshields in local parking lots or dive right into a multi-media campaign, your decisions will be greatly influenced by the budget you have in place. It is critical that advertising have a place in your business plan. A friend once told me that trying to attract customers without advertising is like winking at someone in the dark. You're the only one who knows what you're doing and you're never going to get any results. So, the next time advertising comes up — and you know it will — grab this book instead of an antacid tablet and create an affordable, successful plan for a week or a year!

Introduction

Your business is officially open and, as your first bona fide act of advertising, you list your business phone number — perhaps even a display ad — in the Yellow Pages. This is an important step lending credibility to the business name and giving potential customers reason to feel that yours is a stable company. Flimflam artists who breeze into and out of towns are not known to spend money on Yellow Page ads.

It's also a perfect example of the "camel's nose under the tent." Like your first newspaper ad or first flyer, your Yellow Page ad will result in your being contacted by others wanting you to consider their forms of advertising.

A humble advertising budget forces you to find specific radio stations, television programs, daily and weekly publications, direct mail possibilities, and outdoor advertising that will create interest in your business and bring in the most customers. You are expected to achieve, in whatever amount of time you can squeeze out of your day, a specifically targeted advertising plan without wasting any of your precious advertising dollars in the process.

This is a full time job for advertising executives. It takes knowledge of the market, the ability to read, dissect, and understand market indicators from Arbitron and Neilson, the capacity to creatively attract the attention of audiences, the discipline to meet deadlines, negotiate contracts, and quickly re-evaluate and sometimes revise strategies to deal with changes in the market. How are you supposed to do this in your "spare time" and do it well?

It takes an advertising agency the same amount of time and effort to work with a small client as it does to work with a large one. The same agency employees are involved and the same amount of work has to be done. An ad agency's reputation is always on the line. Its reputation depends on the success of its campaigns. The reality is that the success of a small advertising campaign will be limited simply because the budget cannot support the commercial frequency necessary to generate customer reaction. An advertising agency charges for its work in three different ways:

- Marking up (adding a percent of the cost) work done by outside sources such as printers, typesetters, photographers, etc.

- Charging an hourly fee (which can range from $45.00 an hour for a small agency to hundreds of dollars an hour for a large agency) on creative work, travel, time spent in production or in meetings with or about the client, copy writing, design, etc.

- Commissions (usually 15 percent of the client's budget) based on the placement of any kind of advertising.

Small business owners with modest budgets do not have the luxury of being able to afford the often prohibitive cost of professional help. You must use whatever advertising dollars you have to get the message out — and you have to do it yourself.

Advertising without an agency is not like wallpapering your guest bathroom or landscaping your yard a little each year to save a few dollars. Once you start to advertise, every dollar counts and all aspects of the endeavor become critical immediately.

The good news is that your media sales reps are professionals in advertising, and the really great news is that you don't have to be. The information and worksheets in this book will arm you with the facts necessary to place your advertising dollars where they will do the most good every time. You will learn how to use radio, television, print, direct mail, outdoor advertising, and how to keep track of your decisions (and results) for future reference.

Acknowledgments

Many thanks to the following professionals who kept watch over the accuracy of this information, and made valuable contributions of their own:

Mr. David F. Bellso

Mr. Dick Carr

Mr. Carl Fiorini

Rev. P. V. George

Mr. Francis G. Henke

Mr. Jack Mott

Ms. Carmel Piccoli

Mr. Joseph Salibra

Ms. Theresa Underwood

Mr. Matthew Willis

And my husband Frank, who stood more than once on the shoulder of a very busy highway (in 20 degree weather), photographing billboards.

1

Define Your Market

Most entrepreneurs have had experience as employees of similar businesses and already have a grasp of who their customers should be. It is a good idea, even if you think you know who your customers are, to keep track of them on paper — not only during your first weeks and months, but throughout your business life. Your customer base can change with the addition of services or new merchandise to your inventory, a shift in the community caused by the opening or closing of a university, an industry, a military base, or just the natural aging of people in the community. Throughout this book, I refer to the following groups:

18–34, 18–49, 25–54, 50+   Female   Male   Adults

These are basic demographic age ranges and gender groups used by media to divide the population into manageable segments.

At one time 18–34 was rarely used — a wider range of 18–49 covered the bigger group. However, there is a huge difference in the musical taste of an 18 year old and a 49 year old — the opposite ends of that spectrum — so the 18–34 group was created to break down the larger segment. It allows us to see where the younger portion of that group tunes in and where the older population settles in to listen. The same principle applies to the overlapping of the other groups. As you read along, keep in mind that they do — and are supposed to — overlap. For instance:

- The group 18–34 seems like it could be synonymous with 18–49. But 18–34 represents the younger segment of the two groups, ending a full 15 years short of the larger group. Therefore, a business catering to teens or people in their twenties, would choose to advertise to the 18–34 group rather than choosing the 18–49 group simply because it doesn't want to waste money reaching people too old for its product.

- The 18–49 group fits totally within the 25–54 range. But you will reach the *younger portion of that population segment (ending around age 35)* by using 18–49 and the *older group (35–54)* in the 25–54.

- The same goes for the 25–54 segment and the 50+ group. The 50+ group represents persons age *50 and up* — senior citizens, grandparents, and retired people. While you may reach *some* of these people using 25–54, you would mainly be reaching people too young for your product or service if your major target group is 50+.

While television stations use slightly different age groups, they will fall into the same ranges as the ones listed above. Your television account executives will know exactly which programming best suits your business based on the information you provide.

This chapter provides guidelines for making the correct demographic age and gender choices for your business. Use those guidelines until you get a feel for the process, and keep in mind the "overlap" factor of the groups as you read.

In the advertising and media-buying class I teach, I offer myself as an example of how complex choosing a primary and secondary (even tertiary) demographic group can be. I am a 52 year old female. Businesses catering to 50+ year old females — like those selling cars, clothing, grocery stores, weight-loss clinics and products, vitamins, etc. would know they could send their message to me on the stations and programs catering to the 50+ Female demographic group. Easy, right? Well ...

- I am also a wife and I buy men's clothes. My husband's hobbies include hunting and railroad modeling, so I need to be informed on those topics.

- I am the mother of 3 sons. The oldest works in a bank and is also a hunter. Along with men's clothing, I need to know where to purchase hunting items for birthday and holiday gifts. He was married 2 years ago and that involved me in some of the wedding preparations: balloons, invitations to the rehearsal dinner, flowers, the rehearsal dinner itself, tuxedos, hotel accommodations for our out-of-town guests.

- I love to shop for my daughter-in-law, a teacher by trade, whose hobby is photography. I need to know where and when sales on clothes and shoes for 27-year-old females are happening, and items related to her hobby.

- Last year my husband and I became grandparents and I began purchasing baby clothes, baby furniture, and many other baby items. Perhaps a baby furniture store might not think of me when they are choosing where to spend their advertising dollars — but they should! Another grandbaby is on the way — so they should be looking for me again.

- Son #2 is a police officer who is interested in physical fitness. Again, I need to know about men's clothing — but for a younger demographic than the clothes I buy for my husband. Holiday and birthday gifts for him as well as any regular shopping I do for him includes CDs, lottery subscriptions, small appliances for his apartment. He plays the guitar and likes to go to concerts — things I consider when buying for him.

- Son # 3 is 14 years old. I shop for clothes, movie passes, computer games and programs, video games, school supplies, orthodontist services, and a whole different set of products and services than I deal with for his father and older brothers.

Would you think of advertising to the 50+ Female group for the following items?

- Guitars and accessories
- Baby furniture and baby clothes
- Wedding products and services
- Hunting gear including guns, ammunition, camouflage outerwear, etc.
- Video games
- Clothes and shoes for 25–27 year old women

While I may not be your primary audience, I surely am a strong secondary. You must think very hard about the people you want to reach. Your conclusions will not only guide your decisions on where to consistently place your advertising dollars, but will allow you to take advantage of affordable promotions or advertising packages proposed to you by reps of stations or programs you don't normally consider.

Delivering your message to the right people is the whole story of advertising. The first critical step of determining who the right people are is the one you are about to take. You may find after some thought, that the answer might not be as obvious as you believed.

A car dealer reading this book may go to the next page and circle all of the age choices in Group A because everyone who can drive is a potential customer. Then again, he or she may consider one demographic group for brand new luxury models, another for the more economical models and still another for used cars as the secondary market. Other types of businesses will have a very narrow selection for a primary choice and another very specific group circled for the secondary market.

When you feel you have identified your primary and secondary customers, circle the correct choices from Groups A and B. **You may need to circle more**

than one age choice from Group A. From Group B, you will circle only one option. Does your business lend itself primarily to males, females, or both (in which case you will circle Adults). You will now use this information to identify radio and television stations and publications targeting the groups you have selected. These choices are the basis for all of your media planning and media buying. This is the information from which all advertising decisions are made, so give careful thought to your selections.

Describe your customers by circling the appropriate choices from Groups A and B. You may need to circle more than one choice from Group A.

To simplify the demographic choices you need to make and compensate for the overlapping, use the following guidelines until you develop a feel for the process:

- If you estimate your customers to be 12–24 years of age, circle the 18–34 group.
- If you estimate your customers to be 25–35 years of age, circle the 18–49 group.
- If you estimate your customers to be 36–50 years of age, circle the 25–54 group.
- If you estimate your customers to be over 50 years of age, circle the 50+ group.

Primary Market

Group A (Age)	Group B (Gender)
18–34	Male
18–49	Female
25–54	Adults (Male and Female)
50+	

Secondary Market

Group A (Age)	Group B (Gender)
18–34	Male
18–49	Female
25–54	Adults (Male and Female)
50+	

The Customer Information Worksheet in this section will track changes in your customer base and provide facts you need to make proper advertising decisions. At least twice a year for a 3 or 4 week period, keep these worksheets by your

Customer Information Worksheet

Dates: _____ 9/1/98 _____ to _ 9/4/98 _____

Zip Codes	Gender	Age (estimate)
13219	F	26
13010	F	32
13689	F	20
13219	M	24
13219	F	31
13842	F	35
13209	F	27
13689	M	27
13010	F	30
13219	M	18
13219	F	21
13842	F	24
13219	F	19
13010	M	20
13842	F	21
13010	F	26
13219	M	32
13842	F	30
13010	F	26
	F	21

Zip Codes	Gender		Age	
13219 (7)	Females	15	12–24	9
13010 (5)			25–35	11
13842 (4)	Males	5	36–50	0
13689 (2)			over 50	0
13209 (1)				

register on a clipboard. Ask for each purchaser's zip code, fill in the gender section and estimate the age. Analyzing this information will provide, along with the demographic facts for selecting radio and television stations, the zip code data you need to help you with direct mail and outdoor advertising. It will allow you to evaluate changes in your customer base and respond accordingly.

After each sheet is completed, total the columns and list in order the top 5 zip codes, the number of males and females, and the number of people falling into each age group at the bottom of the page. As you begin analyzing your Customer Information Worksheets, the results will either validate your original assessment of who your customers are or give you a clearer picture of them. If over time the numbers in the columns change, you will be ready to react — not only with your service or product lines, but with your advertising decisions.

A small budget doesn't allow much experimentation, and common sense dictates that you target your primary audience first, then the secondary group. Start by reaching the people closest to your location and then work your way out. Before you finish this book you will read about various forms of advertising that let you be geographically specific as well as demographically specific — such as direct mail, some forms of print, outdoor advertising, and even cable TV.

Tip: Does your business require you to enter customer homes for estimates, cleaning, or installations? Be aware of what station the radio is tuned to or what program is on the television when you are there. Keep a list.

2

Define Yourself

Identifying your business

Today, many business owners create a "mission statement" to summarize the overall purpose of their companies. Simmering down all of the ingredients that make up your product(s) and service(s) into a few written sentences should lead you to the core of your advertising messages. Your mission statement may include personal or industrial convictions (such as Ford's "Quality is Job One"), or a lengthier explanation of what you want your business to mean to the community or the world. Whatever you choose as your mission statement, the exercise of figuring it out will force you to put a lot of thought into your business, the way you will run it, how you regard your customers, the importance you put on your business reputation, and the corporate "feeling" you want to convey to the public. If you wish to be involved with community or with charity work as part of your business routine, figure closely how many hours or dollars you can donate per month or year.

Inventory-rich businesses carry priority products and goods of lesser importance. Make a list of the most critical product lines, brands, and items of high profit return. Service-oriented businesses need to list services in order of importance to the clients, those you have the ability to provide in large quantity, and those with the highest rate of return per hour.

Example: Your kitchen remodeling business may offer three levels of kitchen help: 1) refinishing original cupboards, 2) re-facing original cupboard doors and drawer fronts, 3) installing all new cupboards and offering total kitchen design. You may decide to write your commercials mentioning all three options to reach people interested in all of the services. Or you may highlight only option #1 — the lowest-priced option — to trigger more phone calls — thinking that once you meet with the client you will introduce the other two (more expensive) options.

Can You Diversify?

Ask yourself if there is another branch you can add to your business tree. Diversifying your business from a single-purpose operation cannot only bring in supplemental operating cash, but it can be a business-saver when times get tough for your main business or in a generally poor economic environment.

• Let's say you sell musical instruments and accessories, give music lessons, and do repairs. Can you also set up a small studio where local musicians can come to cut demos? Collect rare instruments and sell them on the Internet? Rent space for local bands to rehearse?

• Do you sell or rent antique furniture, artwork, or used furniture from many periods? It may be possible to rent such items to local theater groups for authentic stage props or to television stations for commercial settings. Could you hold refinishing classes on the weekends or classes on how to discover antiques at garage and tag sales?

• If you sell hunting and fishing equipment, clothing, and accessories, you can make contact with travel agents (or directly with hunting and fishing guides and facilities) to book vacations for your customers. You may be in for a surprise when these facilities invite you to experience what they have to offer for yourself on an all-expense-paid trip. They know that you will sell their facility with enthusiasm if you have first-hand knowledge of the experience.

• Tie your bakery's cakes into family restaurants that provide children's birthday parties or your donuts and pastries into restaurants serving breakfast. Hold classes on cake decorating, wedding etiquette, and even wedding fashion shows to bolster the wedding cake portion of the business. If you have the space, turn it into a decorated "for rent" birthday party room. You can cater as much of the food as you want — just the cakes, breads, and your daily fare, or all of the food.

There are many ways to use your knowledge to branch out from your main business and make it pay. Holding instructional or informational classes, special shows, demonstrations, collector's events, making use of extra space, write a "how-to" book — put on your thinking cap! It's possible the diversification could end up being your biggest money-maker and become your primary business.

Check the Yellow Page display ads of your competitors. See what products or services they highlight — see any diversification going on there? Pay attention to their radio and television commercials, outdoor billboards and print ads. Learn from people in your business who have been around and successful for a long time.

While you're looking at your competitors' ads, think about what products you have or services you can provide that your competitors cannot. Ask yourself why someone should seek you out as opposed to going to one of your competitors? You must have a reason or you are in trouble right from the beginning. Just to tell the public "Hey, here's one more book store, one more shoe store, one more restaurant," is not going to make them check you out. People are creatures of habit and unless you give them something new, exciting, different, better priced, higher quality, etc., they will go where they are used to going for their goods and services. What is your special niche? What's special about your business that makes it worth someone's while to walk through your door?

Don't Overlook the Obvious

A lady went into a pet shop to buy a parrot, as she specifically wanted a bird she could teach to talk. After purchasing a lovely cage, she took the bird home, found a nice sunny spot in her kitchen and introduced the parrot to his new home.

When the parrot would not talk, she went back to the store and bought a swing, thinking the bird needed to be stimulated. But nothing. She went back to the store and bought a mirror for the cage. But the bird would not talk. The woman bought a rope for him to climb and then a little bathtub for him to play in but the parrot said nothing.

One morning she came down to the kitchen and found the bird lying on its back on the bottom of the cage with his tiny feet sticking straight up in the air. Horrified, she picked it up and held it in her hand. With its last little gasps, the parrot finally spoke to her, "Don't they sell any food down there?"

Sometimes the simple basics are overlooked. And one basic fact is that there's no advertising in the world that can replace a favorable direct contact with your product or service. For example, if you have a bakery, a bagelry, a restaurant, a sandwich shop, a pretzel stand — anything to do with food — take free samples to radio personalities in your area. Make up trays of bagels or baked goods and deliver them early one morning as a surprise. The staff will enjoy them all through the day. If you're treating them to a hot or cold lunch, call the day before so you won't walk into an empty building at lunch time. Put a sign, a business card, or a menu with the tray or food containers. Chances are, your business will be mentioned several times throughout the day by grateful show hosts. Then start delivering trays of baked goods, bagels, sandwiches, or "finger foods" to businesses in your area.

If you want to expand your regular breakfast and lunch business into take-out or delivery, leave several flyers along with the trays of food. Include your menu, prices, and phone and fax numbers. Take food and flyers to every large business in your delivery area. Let them know you cater conference room lunches and office parties if you do. Many businesses and agencies hold monthly board meetings with a catered lunch. You can pick up regular contractual business this way.

Suggest in your flyers that people order ahead and pick up dinner on the way home or baked goods for tomorrow's breakfast. It will sound like a great idea to folks who are tired from a long day at the office and not particularly looking forward to cooking when they get home. Show the benefit of your product or service and you will get results.

Hair salons and clothing stores provide clothes, hair and nail care, and makeup to television news people in return for credit during news casts.

If your product or service does not lend itself to free sampling, target businesses in your area where large numbers of people are cooped up all day and deliver coupons worth 50 percent off lunchtime exercise or diet programs, home gym equipment, motorcycles, skis, fishing equipment, boats, convertibles, decks, gas grilles, pool and patio furniture, or a luxury weekend get-away. Even swimming pools or Jacuzzis — anything that will sound good to someone trapped in an office 8–10 hours a day.

Any product or service that you donate in this way can be written off as a business expense under "advertising" because that is precisely what you are doing. Check with an accountant for applicable tax codes in your area.

Envision the daily life of your target consumers. Every moment from the time they wake up to the time they go back to bed. Where would your product or service fit in? What problem would it solve? What benefit can you show that will make that person believe your product or service is not a desire, but a necessity? If it solves a financial problem, makes the neighbors jealous, provides a health-related improvement, gives a psychological or physical boost, gives an edge or an advantage over a competitor, whatever the benefit may be — show it, say it, make them believe it — and you've got a sale. Don't be afraid to seek them out — it isn't necessary, or even advisable, to wait for them to find you.

Gift certificates are a great way to increase your business. Don't buy stock certificates right off the shelf. They're too easy to duplicate. Use specialty paper and make one or two identifying marks on the certificates so you can verify authenticity when one is brought to you for redemption. Gift certificates allow you to keep more inventory in the store during peak shopping times, and some of the certificates you sell will never be redeemed.

Creative opportunities to "show your stuff" are everywhere. You know your product(s) or service(s) better than anyone and you know who your target consumers are. Find out where they are and go after them with radio, television, print, outdoor, and direct mail advertising, and direct contact!

Whatcha Gonna Say, How're Ya Gonna Say It?

If you watch late night television, you've no doubt seen Jay Leno holding up amusing newspaper headlines or photos with captions. Because of a typographical error or incorrect use of a word, the messages ended up being far from what the writers had actually intended to say or imply. This is an important lesson! A notice similar to the following one, posted on a church bulletin board, unfortunately read:

> Tonight's weight loss clinic will be held in the social hall at 8 PM.
> Please use the large double doors at the side of the building to enter.

Read every line you write and read every line someone else writes for you — be it a script, copy for a merchandise bag, or a coupon — that goes out with your business name and/or logo on it! One misspelled word, one misplaced word, one misused word can mean disaster! Think ahead! It's sound advice in business life as well as in regular life. Just ask Mr. Benjamin Dover if he ever wished his parents had given serious thought as to whether his friends might ever call him Ben. Go ahead — say it — Ben Dover.

A small but elegant shop in my community specializing in beautiful greeting cards, put items purchased into colorful little merchandise bags. On the bags were the words, "Where quality and value goes hand in hand." This message was printed on bags used by a greeting card company — where the message literally means business! I mentioned to the clerk that she might want to bring the error to her manager's attention, and within two or three months new bags appeared with the message "Where quality and value go hand in hand." And one of my favorite stories concerned a small furniture store that started competing against larger department stores by carrying a line of higher-quality brands. The store's ad read:

We've upped our image! Up Yours!

While your letterhead, business cards, and merchandise bags carry the same basic copy to everyone, you can actively appeal to specific demographic groups with properly written and properly placed radio, television, and print ads.

While some businesses cater to a very specific clientele, others offer products with a more universal appeal such as automobile dealers, music stores, grocery stores, gas stations, insurance companies, health clinics, pet shops, just to name a few. If your business can attract customers or clients from more than one specific group, you can take advantage of special deals that may come along within almost any category of advertising. Let me give you some examples.

Example #1: Every automobile dealer carries many different models — from two-seater convertible sports cars, to station wagons, to four-door family models, to 10-passenger vans, to plush top-of-the-line, high-end luxury sedans. A company like this can advertise to anyone old enough to drive! What an opportunity to take advantage of special promotions and deals from almost any station in existence. By simply writing separate scripts featuring the appropriate vehicle to attract the 18–34 crowd, the 25–54 gang and the 50+ bunch, this business owner can target all drivers.

The results can be enhanced with print ads showing pictures of the various vehicles described in your commercials. Place the ads in publications that match the demographics groups of your radio and television schedule.

Example #2: A musical instrument shop specializing in the sale of guitars, harmonicas, and drums, and also providing music lessons, might use late night television hoping to attract musicians who get home from work very late and sleep during the day. Or they might use a radio station with a Male 18–34 demographic hoping to sell instruments to high school kids interested in putting their own bands together. But why couldn't they also use a radio station catering to the parents of these teens? While a young man or woman may want a flashy electric guitar, how many of them actually have the cash to buy one? Often it's the parents who come up with a portion or all of the money for these big-ticket items. And might not those same parents also have younger children who could benefit from music lessons? These parents would be found on a station catering to Adults 25–54. And wait a minute — what about grandparents who may think that their grandson or granddaughter is a musical genius? Again, as we saw with the automobile dealer, there is not only one but many possible groups a store such as this might target. Could this shop, with properly written copy, place an ad on stations with audiences full of Males 18–34, or Adults 25–54, or Adults 50+? Let's see:

:30 second radio script (targeting Males 18–34) Client/The Music Bed

Instructions: Use hard rock music and young male voice w/ highly energetic read.

GET YOUR BUTT DOWN TO THE MUSIC BED FOR A WEEK-LONG BLOW OUT SALE AND GET THE LOWEST PRICES AVAILABLE ANYWHERE ON THE HOTTEST ELECTRIC GUITARS IN THE COUNTRY! WHETHER YOU'RE ROCKIN' PROFESSIONALLY OR JUST GETTIN' YOUR

GROUP TOGETHER, THE MUSIC BED HAS EVERYTHING
YOU NEED. ACCESSORIES ALL HALF PRICE TIL SUNDAY!
THE MUSIC BED — LOCATED AT 123 FOURTH STREET —
IS THE PLACE FOR PEOPLE WHO MAKE IT HAPPEN!
SHOW UP TODAY!

:30 second radio script (targeting Adults 25–54) Client/The Music Bed

Instructions: Use middle-aged male or female teacher-type voice, and upbeat music. Break in SFX of squeaking violin, off-key horn, etc. where indicated by ★★

THE MUSIC BED ★★ IS HAVING A WEEK-LONG SALE —
WITH THE LOWEST PRICES AVAILABLE ON ELECTRIC
AND ACOUSTIC GUITARS, DRUMS, HARMONICAS AND
ACCESSORIES. THE MUSIC BED OFFERS AFFORDABLE ★★
LESSONS — AND THE FIRST TWO LESSONS ARE FREE
WHEN YOU SIGN UP FOR TEN! BRING YOUR BUDDING
MUSICIAN ★★ TO THE MUSIC BED THIS WEEK AND LET
OUR PROFESSIONAL MUSICIANS HELP YOU SELECT THE
INSTRUMENT THAT FITS YOUR BUDGET AS WELL AS
YOUR CHILD. THE MUSIC BED, 123 FOURTH STREET. ★★

:30 second radio script (targeting Adults 50+) Client/The Music Bed

Instructions: Use kindly older male or female voice — as if speaking to a friend. Background soft SFX of squeaking violin, off key horn, etc. where indicated by ★★

INTRODUCE YOUR MUSICALLY GIFTED GRANDCHILD
TO AN EXCITING MUSICAL INSTRUMENT ★★ AND
LESSONS (THE FIRST TWO LESSONS ARE FREE WHEN
YOU SIGN UP FOR TEN!) RIGHT NOW THE MUSIC BED IS
HAVING A WEEK-LONG SALE ON ELECTRIC AND
ACOUSTIC GUITARS, DRUMS, HARMONICAS AND KEY-
BOARDS. BRING YOUR FAVORITE ★★ BUDDING MUSI-
CIAN TO THE MUSIC BED THIS WEEK AND SELECT AN
INSTRUMENT THAT FITS YOUR BUDGET AS WELL AS
YOUR GRANDCHILD. THE MUSIC BED, 123 FOURTH
STREET. ★★

Now let's turn them into television scripts you could run at the same time. The television script is divided into two sections, audio and video, so that you can tell what the audience will see as well as hear. Using your produced radio commercials for the television audio keeps the sound effects, voices, and background music constant and more easily recognized. Just ask your radio rep for a copy of the commercial for your television production.

:30 second script (targeting Males 18–34) Client/The Music Bed

AUDIO	VIDEO
Get your butt down to the Music Bed for a week-long blow-out sale and get the lowest prices available anywhere on the hottest electric guitars in the country!	Shot of store exterior Photos of various styles of guitars on display
Whether you're rockin' professionally or just gettin' your group together, the Music Bed has everything you need. Accessories all half price 'til Sunday!	Show selection of guitar straps, picks, music, etc.
The Music Bed! Located at 123 Fourth Street — is the place for people who make things happen! Show up today!	Shot of business exterior sign, location & phone # 18–25 year olds holding guitars, yelling this line at the camera.

:30 second script (targeting Adults 25–54) Client/The Music Bed

AUDIO	VIDEO
The Music Bed is having a week-long sale with the lowest prices available on electric and acoustic guitars, drums, harmonicas, and accessories.	Shot of store exterior.
The Music Bed offers affordable lessons and the first two lessons are free when you sign up for ten!	Shot of parent walking the child into or through store looking at different instruments.

AUDIO	VIDEO
Bring your budding musician to The Music Bed this week and let our professional musicians help you select the instrument that fits your budget as well as your child. The Music Bed, 123 Fourth Street	Shot of children (looking happy) Parent getting hug from happy child. Store exterior, logo, phone #.

:30 second script (targeting Adults 50+) Client/The Music Bed

AUDIO	VIDEO
Introduce your musically gifted grandchild to an exciting musical instrument and lessons! The first two lessons are free when you sign up for ten.	Store exterior. Grandparent and child walking through store looking at instruments.
Right now the Music Bed is having a week-long sale on electric and acoustic guitars, drums, harmonicas, and keyboards.	Shot of instruments on display.
Bring your favorite budding musician to the Music Bed this week and select an instrument that fits your budget as well as your grandchild.	Child taking lessons while grandparent looks on. (Child looks happy). Grandparent getting hug from happy child.
The Music Bed, 123 Fourth Street	Exterior shot of store. Logo and Phone #.

Keep the original copies — not VHS tapes and cassettes — the original master copies of all radio and television commercials. Label each one with the information shown on the sample label on the next page. Store all master copies in a designated cool, dry area so that you will know right where they are if you want to use them again. Write the title of the commercial and the date of production on the label, and keep a typed script of the spot in the box or attached to the box with a rubber band. Then you can read the script at a future date to check for any outdated information. This is especially important when you consider the cost of television production. But it also serves as a convenience if you have either radio or television commercials that have worked for you in the past and you wish to re-use them instead of re-write them.

❏ Radio   ❏ Television

Length ❏ :10   ❏ :30   ❏ :60

Title: _____

Date: _____

Logo Development

As a small or new business you may not have the funds to hire an artist or a graphic artist to develop a logo — it can cost thousands of dollars! But expensive and original graphics are not necessary to create an identifying look for your business sign, cards, letterhead, contracts, etc. Look in the Yellow Pages of your local phone book for a typesetter or printer. They will help you select fonts (styles of lettering), shading, color(s), and any number of other additions you might like to create your own special look.

Along with font style and color, you will want to consider how much your logo can say about the purpose of your business. For instance, my advertising agency, Silent Partner Advertising, does a lot of behind-the-scenes work, where we actually are responsible for special events, business development, advertising, and facilitating services for other companies. We are not at all in the spotlight, and do not receive credit (or blame) at the end — so the name Silent Partner "fits." The handshake on our logo alludes to an agreement or partnership. I use a business-like burgundy ink on a gray linen paper for my formal letterhead, envelopes, and business cards. But for informal letters and envelopes, invoices, and some contracts, I use simple, less expensive (also burgundy-colored) lettering on white paper. My logo is shown below:

Silent Partner Advertising
106 Peridot Drive
Syracuse, NY 13219

(Times New Roman)

The colors I have chosen may not be as effective for a garden shop or landscape business, where shades of green with pink, red, or yellow ink on a pastel-colored paper would create the right feeling.

To give you an idea of how you can create an identifying look with a particular font, I have shown my business name in several types and the names of each one. There are literally thousands to choose from:

Silent Partner Advertising
106 Peridot Drive
Syracuse, NY 13219

(Signet Roundhand A)

Silent Partner Advertising
106 Peridot Drive
Syracuse, NY 13219

(Snowdrift)

SILENT PARTNER ADVERTISING
106 PERIDOT DRIVE
SYRACUSE, NY 13219

(Bazooka)

Silent Partner Advertising
106 Peridot Drive
Syracuse, NY 13219

(Courier New)

Silent Partner Advertising
106 Peridot Drive
Syracuse, NY 13219

(Cricket)

Silent Partner Advertising
106 Peridot Drive
Syracuse, 13219

(Aristocrat)

Silent Partner Advertising
106 Peridot Drive
Syracuse, NY 13219

(Geometric)

SILENT PARTNER ADVERTISING
106 PERIDOT DRIVE
SYRACUSE, NY 13219

(Creepy)

Silent Partner Advertising
106 Peridot Drive
Syracuse, NY 13219

(University)

Silent Partner Advertising
106 Peridot Drive
Syracuse, NY 13219

(Braggadocio)

SILENT PARTNER ADVERTISING
106 PERIDOT DRIVE
SYRACUSE NY 13219

(Boxed In)

Silent Partner Advertising
106 Peridot Drive
Syracuse, NY 13219

(Benguiat Book)

Silent Partner Advertising
106 Peridot Drive
Syracuse, NY 13219

(Book Antiqua)

Silent Partner Advertising
106 Peridot Drive
Syracuse, NY 13219

(Bookman Light)

SILENT PARTNER ADVERTISING
106 PERIDOT DRIVE
SYRACUSE, NY 13219

(Encino)

Silent Partner Advertising
106 Peridot Drive
Syracuse, NY 13219

(Torino Outline)

SILENT PARTNER ADVERTISING
106 PERIDOT DRIVE
SYRACUSE, NY 13219

(Halloween)

Consider the name of your business, your products, services, etc. and then find a font that looks like it fits. For instance, a Halloween costume shop might do well with the fonts "Creepy" or "Halloween" — while a funeral director would want to stay away from the font "Boxed In."

If you choose such a font, use it only for the name of the business and go with an easier-to-read font for your address, phone number and your own name if it appears on the card as shown here:

THE MASQUERADE SHOPPE
1234 Alphabet Avenue
Albany, NY 12345
Mr. Paul Smith (333) 555-2222

Use a larger font for the business name in bold so it will stand out from the other information on the card. Each font is available in a very small to a very large size to allow you maximum flexibility is designing your logo.

M M M M M M M

Try different combinations until you find a design that's visually pleasing and gives an accurate impression of your business. You can find clip art books and computer software in almost any store carrying business or art supplies. If you would like more than distinctive lettering as part of your logo, use artwork found in these sources to add some extra interest. Later, when you have the funds available, go ahead and call a graphic artist. Clip art and many of the fonts you see in this book are available on any word processing program.

Your business logo will become more and more recognizable as time goes on — especially if you've put a lot of thought into making it unique. Use it everywhere — on everything you print. There should never be an envelope, piece of letterhead, Yellow Page ad, print ad, outdoor billboard, contract, invoice, or merchandise bag that leaves your company without your logo on it.

Push it further and consider using your logo colors to paint the outside of your front door and around your windows if you're in a free-standing shop or having your logo etched into the glass portion of your door if you're within a business complex. The more it's seen, the faster it will become recognizable. You want a logo that will stand out in an ad, in a pile of mail, a pile of invoices, or a pile of business cards.

There is nothing more boring and less inspiring than a business card with a few lines of black print on a white background. Even the most buttoned-down, laidback, let's say, accounting firm (sorry) can have a handsome (but not creative — a word accounting firms probably don't want to be associated with), dignified, interesting logo.

Ask your printer for samples of other business cards. They will have hundreds to show you. Look at and feel different stocks and weights of paper to find the one you want. After all, when you hand out a business card, it may be the only tangible reminder the person has of you and your business days, weeks, or months after your meeting. Make it memorable! If you are not particularly good or interested in design and color, ask a friend or family member who has some talent in that area to go with you to help make choices.

You can have Rolodex cards made up with your business name on the tab. They are easy to file and make it simple for that customer or client to find your phone, fax, and E-mail numbers in a hurry. The easier you make it for people to find you and do business with you, the more successful you will be.

Press Release

One of the first things an entrepreneur wants to do is make a public announcement that the business exists and is open. But what do you say?

Very few local publications will print a press release just because you write it and send it in. OK, so maybe they are not as excited as you are about your new endeavor. Find an angle that will make them interested. A good title is a great place to start. If you study the regular articles in your daily or weekly papers, you'll see that the titles of the articles are written to attract the reader's attention. How many times have you stood in line at a grocery or drugstore and read something as outrageous as, "Sneeze blows hair off man's head!" as a title on the cover of a magazine — only to find out that a woman sneezed while standing behind her husband and his toupee moved a little?

Use some creativity, though not tabloid in nature, to grab the reader's attention. If the first reader is the editor of the local business section, you may have a good chance of seeing your press release in print. Look for an interesting angle, an off-beat, comical, or ironic twist. Create your press release with the reader in mind. Make it short, interesting, and above all, give it a catchy title:

Popcorn King Buys Local Theater for Peanuts!

Many weekly community papers have a feature called "Business of the Week" or "Business Person of the Week." You'll have an easier time getting into that feature — at least in the edition that covers your geographic area — especially if you do a little paid advertising in the publication now and again. Make a call to the editor and ask! Supply the newspaper with a photo of you in front of your location. Color shots do not always reprint well into a black and white format, so put together some black and white photos of you and/or your business for opportunities that come along.

If something interesting in the daily news corresponds to the work you do, call your local television stations, radio stations, and newspapers to let them know you are willing to be interviewed as an expert for pertinent information or to give a professional opinion on the subject at hand now or in the future.

Tip: Start advertising your seasonal business earlier then you normally would to increase name awareness and "mind-share" over your competitors.

3

Media Sales Reps

Media sales representatives, a.k.a. account executives, are among the most friendly, good humored, persuasive people you will meet in your career as a business owner. You will find it easy to become friends with many of them, and easy to be flattered by the attention they give, the lunches and concert tickets they can provide. If all goes well, you will enjoy the time you spend with those who represent the stations and publications you need. Your media account executives work within an ever-changing environment. Competition and change are the two constants in the world of media sales. Market forces, changes in station ratings, unacceptable sales performance, and many other factors can cause sales reps to move, voluntarily or otherwise, from one employer to another.

It can be difficult to see a favorite sales rep who has been calling on you from radio station A suddenly show up at your door as an energetic rep from radio station B and later yet as a sales rep from the daily newspaper. You can start to wonder about his or her objectivity and question any advertising advice you may have received from that rep in the past. It may be the first time you see this person as a sales representative whose goal it is to persuade you to do business with whatever station or publication he or she represents. As friendly and fun as they can be, media reps are working tirelessly to meet tough budgets and will try hard to dissuade you from placing your advertising dollars elsewhere. It is what they are trained to do.

Every sales staff is trained differently. The type of training can be directly linked to the size and financial condition of the company they work for. For instance, radio and television stations with large audiences, high ratings, and therefore high rates, are able to send their sales people to fairly lavish training sessions and hire expensive consultants to hone and perfect every sales skill.

Stations with small audiences and lower operating budgets (since the two are hopelessly intertwined) cannot afford that level of extravagance and will rely on a sharp, experienced sales manager to work with each individual account executive as well as with the group as a whole to be creative and competent in the field. Managers of both kinds of stations will put together promotion-oriented packages hoping to draw you in with the excitement of a big event. Both sales teams learn the art of cold calling, although smaller stations will do more of it by necessity. In most markets you will find a high percentage of the media reps to be professional and knowledgeable.

Radio and television sales people quickly learn how to interpret the ratings of his or her station and how to put the best light on its current standing in the market. After each new "book" has arrived, it is the job of each rep to put the best spin on whatever Arbitron or Nielsen had to say. Trust me when I tell you that each station in the market can and will come up with a plausible case for you to cough up your advertising dollars. The case may be made because of the numbers and it may also be made in spite of the numbers.

Radio and television have, at certain times of the year (like 1st quarter), a lot of inventory to fill, and at other times, are sold out. It's interesting that while most radio reps will say "We're sold out," to a client who called too late, television stations actually "bump" clients who are already booked for clients who will pay higher rates for their spots. Bidding wars for space is not uncommon in television. One of my clients was bumped (or as my television rep likes to say — preempted — it sounds nicer) this week. To the television station's credit, they offered to move my client to a higher-priced program (with the same demographic audience) and gave us double the amount of commercials we had originally booked — with no increase in price. Check out the following visual to see what these reps have to sell — and occasionally fill to the brim:

At an average 12 messages per half hour during a Monday - Friday week, this is what a 5 AM to midnight day looks like at a television station. (38 half hours = 456 commercials per day). Each "X" = 1 commercial.

```
X X X X X X X X X X X X X X X X X X X X X X X X
X X X X X X X X X X X X X X X X X X X X X X X X
X X X X X X X X X X X X X X X X X X X X X X X X
X X X X X X X X X X X X X X X X X X X X X X X X
X X X X X X X X X X X X X X X X X X X X X X X X
X X X X X X X X X X X X X X X X X X X X X X X X
X X X X X X X X X X X X X X X X X X X X X X X X
X X X X X X X X X X X X X X X X X X X X X X X X
X X X X X X X X X X X X X X X X X X X X X X X X
```

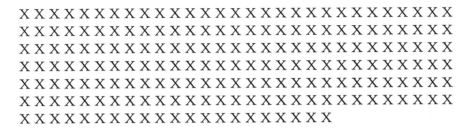

Remember that this represents only one day from 5 AM to midnight. It might be interesting for you at this point to see how many commercials you think you might need to place in one day on one television station to get your message on enough to be seen and heard through all the others. Say you purchase a weekly (Monday to Friday) schedule of 20 commercials, giving you 5 commercials per day. Circle any 5 Xs on the grid above and see how you feel about that schedule's chance of being received.

Even more interesting, circle any 20 Xs below to see how your entire weekly schedule looks. A total week averaging 456 spots for a 5 AM to midnight, Monday through Friday = 2,280 openings, looks approximately as follows:

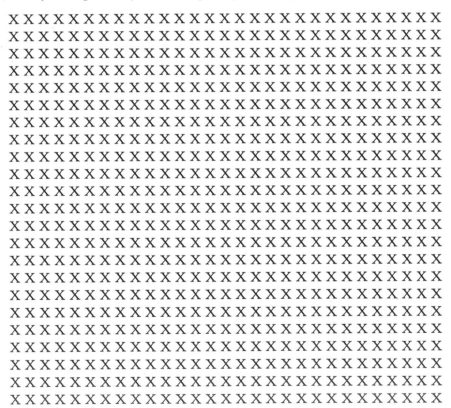

X X X X X X X X X X X X X X X X X X X X X X X X X X X X X X
X X X X X X X X X X X X X X X X X X X X X X X X X X X X X X
X X X X X X X X X X X X X X X X X X X X X X X X X X X X X X
X X X X X X X X X X X X X X X X X X X X X X X X X X X X X X
X X X X X X X X X X X X X X X X X X X X X X X X X X X X X X
X X X X X X X X X X X X X X X X X X X X X X X X X X X X X X
X X X X X X X X X X X X X X X X X X X X X X X X X X X X X X
X X X X X X X X X X X X X X X X X X X X X X X X X X X X X X
X X X X X X X X X X X X X X X X X X X X X X X X X X X X X X
X X X X X X X X X X X X X X X X X X X X X X X X X X X X X X
X X X X X X X X X X X X X X X X X X X X X X X X X X X X X X
X X X X X X X X X X X X X X X X X X X X X X X X X X X X X X
X X X X X X X X X X X X X X X X X X X X X X X X X X X X X X
X X X X X X X X X X X X X X X X X X X X X X X X X X X X X X
X X X X X X X X X X X X X X X X X X X X X X X X X X X X X X
X X X X X X X X X X X X X X X X X X X X X X X X X X X X X X
X X X X X X X X X X X X X X X X X X X X X X X X X X X X X X
X X X X X X X X X X X X X X X X X X X X X X X X X X X X X X
X X X X X X X X X X X X X X X X X X X X X X X X X X X X X X
X X X X X X X X X X X X X X X X X X X X X X X X X X X X X X
X X X X X X X X X X X X X X X X X X X X X X X X X X X X X X
X X X X X X X X X X X X X X X X X X X X X X X X X X X X X X
X X X X X X X X X X X X X X X X X X X X X X X X X X X X X X
X X X X X X X X X X X X X X X X X X X X X X X X X X X X X X
X X X X X X X X X X X X X X X X X X X X X X X X X X X X X X
X X X X X X X X X X X X X X X X X X X X X X X X X X X X X X
X X X X X X X X X X X X X X X X X X X X X X X X X X X X X X
X X X X X X X X X X X X X X X X X X X X X X X X X X X X X X
X X X X X X X X X X X X X X X X X X X X X X X X X X X X X X
X X X X X X X X X X X X X X X X X X X X X X X X X X X X X X
X X X X X X X X X X X X X X X X X X X X X X X X X X X X X X
X X X X X X X X X X X X X X X X X X X X X X X X X X X X X X
X X X X X X X X X X X X X X X X X X X X X X X X X X X X X X
X X X X X X X X X X X X X X X X X X X X X X X X X X X X X X
X X X X X X X X X X X X X X X X X X X X X X X X X X X X X X
X X X X X X X X X X X X X X X X X X X X X X X X X X X X X X
X X X X X X X X X X X X X X X X X X X X X X X X X X X X X

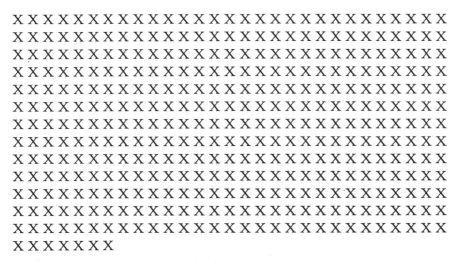

Weekends can have more openings yet. Now, not every X showing has to literally be filled by television account executives. Programs comes to the stations with some commercials already inserted into the breaks and some openings they can fill with local clients. However, you must consider every X when thinking about how many commercials you should run to get your message through to your audience. The television section of this book covers what may seem to be an impossible task — how to place your television commercials effectively.

The overwhelming majority of television commercials are :30 seconds in length, and :60 second spots cost more. In radio, however, commercials are not sold at different prices, rather they are sold as "units" so you can buy a :30 or a :60 second commercial for the same price.

For an FM radio station, there are an average of 8 openings per hour — during a 5 AM to midnight day and 10 openings for the same period of time on an AM station. (Average because you will find a few less per hour from 5 AM to 9 AM and a couple more openings per hour from 9 AM to midnight). This equals 152 openings per day on an FM station and 190 per day on an AM station. It looks like this:

```
X X X X X X X X X X X X X X X X X X X X X X X X X X X X
X X X X X X X X X X X X X X X X X X X X X X X X X X X X
X X X X X X X X X X X X X X X X X X X X X X X X X X X X
X X X X X X X X X X X X X X X X X X X X X X X X X X X X
X X X X X X X X X X X X X X X X X X X X X X X X X X X X
X X X X X X X X X X X X X X X X X X X X X X X X X X X X
X X X X X X X X X X X X X X X X
```

Over a 7 day week the number of openings looks like this: Circle any 24 Xs and see what your message must break through when you place a schedule of 24 commercials.

```
X X X X X X X X X X X X X X X X X X X X X X X X X X
X X X X X X X X X X X X X X X X X X X X X X X X X X
X X X X X X X X X X X X X X X X X X X X X X X X X X
X X X X X X X X X X X X X X X X X X X X X X X X X X
X X X X X X X X X X X X X X X X X X X X X X X X X X
X X X X X X X X X X X X X X X X X X X X X X X X X X
X X X X X X X X X X X X X X X X X X X X X X X X X X
X X X X X X X X X X X X X X X X X X X X X X X X X X
X X X X X X X X X X X X X X X X X X X X X X X X X X
X X X X X X X X X X X X X X X X X X X X X X X X X X
X X X X X X X X X X X X X X X X X X X X X X X X X X
X X X X X X X X X X X X X X X X X X X X X X X X X X
X X X X X X X X X X X X X X X X X X X X X X X X X X
X X X X X X X X X X X X X X X X X X X X X X X X X X
X X X X X X X X X X X X X X X X X X X X X X X X X X
X X X X X X X X X X X X X X X X X X X X X X X X X X
X X X X X X X X X X X X X X X X X X X X X X X X X X
X X X X X X X X X X X X X X X X X X X X X X X X X X
X X X X X X X X X X X X X X X X X X X X X X X X X X
X X X X X X X X X X X X X X X X X X X X X X X X X X
X X X X X X X X X X X X X X X X X X X X X X X X X X
X X X X X X X X X X X X X X X X X X X X X X X X X X
X X X X X X X X X X X X X X X X X X X X X X X X X X
X X X X X X X X X X X X X X X X X X X X X X X X X X
X X X X X X X X X X X X X X X X X X X X X X X X X X
X X X X X X X X X X X X X X X X X X X X X X X X X X
X X X X X X X X X X X X X X X X X X X X X X X X X X
X X X X X X X X X X X X X X X X X X X-X X X X X X X X X
X X X X X X X X X X X X X X X X X X X X X X X X X X
X X X X X X X X X X X X X X X X X X X X X X X X X X
X X X X X X X X X X X X X X X X X X X X X X X X X X
X X X X X X X X X X X X X X X X X X X X X X X X X X
X X X X X X X X X X X X X X X X X X X X X X X X X X
X X X X X X X X X X X X X X X X X X X X X X X X X X
X X X X X X X X X X X X X X X X X X X X X X X X X X
X X X X X X X X X X X X X X X X X X X X X X X X X X
X X X X X X X X X X X X X X X X X X X X X X X X X X
X X X X X X X X X X X X X X X X X X X X X X X X X X
X X X X X X X X X X X X X X X X X X X X X X X X X X
```

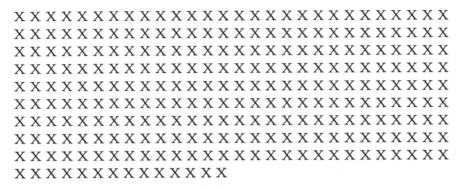

Luckily, you don't need a lot of these Xs to have a good advertising schedule. Some of them wouldn't do you any good at all while others are critical. You need to know which Xs you need and which you don't to place your advertising efficiently. The Radio and Television sections of this book will show you how to place your schedules effectively even though there may be 30 – 50 or more radio stations and several television stations (plus cable) to choose from in your area — each with more Xs than you could stand to think about!

Competition is keen between radio and television, and more so between competing stations of the same kind (for example, radio vs. radio, television vs. television — including network vs. cable TV).

You may find that dealing with your print, direct mail, and outdoor advertising account executives is a little more relaxed although there will still be competition between daily and weekly papers and between competing dailies if you're lucky enough to have more than one in your area.

There will never be as large a number of competing direct mail and outdoor companies or publications in one market as there are competing radio and television stations. Although these reps are also calling on you with the intent of capturing your advertising dollars, they do not have as much individual competition to sell against once they have your interest. The most difficult part of their job is to sway you away from the glitz and glamour of radio and television in general, and toward their particular *type* of media.

Advertising in different forms of print such as dailies, weeklies, shoppers, and magazines does not require the same amount of effort as radio and television. Some decisions are very easy because they are strictly budgetary. Weeklies and shoppers are less expensive than daily newspapers. Many new business owners find that when the dailies are out of reach, the smaller papers offer a great place to start. Chapter 6 covers all of these forms of print, how to advertise geographically with print, how to make your ads stand out from the competition, and which types of print work best for high- and low-ticket products and services.

Then you have to consider Direct Mail — a great way to reach a lot of people or just those in specific zip codes. Coupons and flyers do very well (especially for certain types of businesses) and there are different ways to design them, send them out, and pay for them. Chapter 7 covers these great little "missiles of the mail" and shows you how and when to use them to increase traffic in your store.

Outdoor advertising is an interesting form of advertising and includes outdoor billboards and transit (signs on buses) advertising. When you advertise outdoors, there is no difference in impact for a one-location business than there is for a national business with a multi-million dollar advertising budget. Outdoor billboards come in 3 sizes — that's it — so a bigger company can't buy a bigger board. A larger budget allows more signs, but not bigger signs. The same goes for transit advertising. The signs come in several sizes and everyone has the same choice. Outdoor is where your new business can look as good as a huge company!

Chapters 8 and 9 go into the details of design, contracts, how to be geographically specific and how to make a big splash all day long, day-after-day, with one buy.

One of the first questions all reps will ask is, "What budget are you working with?" Whether you believe it or not, they are not asking this to determine what their commission will be. A good rep knows that a very small budget with low frequency — be it print or electronic — will not produce the desired results and will be hesitant to run a schedule almost certainly doomed to failure. That scenario always ends up with a disappointed business owner and a rep who has little chance of a continuing relationship. The station or paper looks ineffective and will probably not be used again by the client.

Once you decide to work with any rep, from radio, television, print, outdoor, or direct mail, be sure to provide an accurate budget figure so he or she can put together a realistic proposal for you — and don't hold back. If you can spend $8 to $10 thousand in one week, then say it! You wouldn't expect a real estate agent to find you a house without knowing what you can afford to spend. It's exactly the same with advertising. The possible combinations are too overwhelming to put down on paper without knowing what you can afford.

If you are planning to put together your media buy *after* you accept proposals from all of your reps, let that be known. Then they will know that (1) they have to share the total budget and (2) each rep will work to give you the best deal possible to entice you to place a large share of your budget with him or her.

The professional media account executive understands every aspect of his or her business. The production people, on-air personalities, and art directors have their own areas of expertise, as do the people in traffic, news, and promotion departments — but they take little or no interest in the sales department. But the sales reps know every aspect of each of those areas as well as their own. Most of your reps are hard working professionals who truly care that your advertising works for you. Not only will successful media campaigns mean repeat business for them, but they enjoy and take pride in helping your business to grow. They will be listening closely to whatever you tell them about your business, so be sure you provide the most accurate information possible.

Most of the time you will get along with your media sales reps. If you should end up with a personality clash, call the station or publication manager and request a new sales person. It happens. And most places will be more than happy to honor your request. Because nothing in life goes smoothly forever, avoid unpleasant situations down the road by keeping relationships with your media sales reps on a pleasant, but strictly business basis. It makes it a whole lot easier to deal with problems that may arise or to say "no" to that favorite salesperson from radio station A, a station you need, when he shows up selling radio station B, a station you do not need. When filled out properly, your worksheets will contain all of the decision-making information you need to say yes or no to any sales representative, taking it out of the personal arena altogether.

If your business is to succeed, you must be a great salesperson. Observe and listen to your media sales reps. You can learn a lot from the good ones who are great enough at what they do — to do anything — and choose to be your media sales representative.

Tip: Don't buy a station because you like the rep or because it's your favorite. And don't consider investing in any advertising or promotion with any station or publication unless you know it targets your desired audience.

Tip: If you include a self-addressed stamped return envelope with every invoice you mail, your clients will pay their bills faster.

Interns

If you find yourself wearing too many hats and without adequate funds to hire enough people to fill the demand, look to your local college and university intern programs for help. Many Junior and Senior students are waiting on lists in those programs for businesses in the community to give them a hands-on opportunity to use everything they've learned. All it takes is a phone call and a few minutes to fill out a form giving some information about your business and stating the kind of intern you're looking for. You can host students who will help in advertising, accounting, merchandising, purchasing, marketing. You name it, you can probably find an intern to help.

You, or the head of the department in which your intern will work, must have expertise in the career field of the intern you plan to host. This is a MUST for supervision and evaluation purposes. In turn, you are providing a meaningful real-world work setting for someone who has learned a great deal from lectures and books, but needs hands-on experience. And the student will find it valuable to add this work to his or her resume for subsequent job hunting.

The intern's work hours should suit both your business needs and his or her school schedule. At approximately mid-point in the semester, the sponsoring college or university will contact you regarding the intern's progress. While you may not be required to pay a weekly salary (although some do pay interns on a voluntary basis), you will need to keep track of his or her hours and performance, as this student will receive a grade for this internship based primarily on these reports. I usually reward an intern who has done a good job with a check or gift certificate at the end of his or her semester and the offer of a positive reference letter when it's needed for a job. Internships are a natural opportunity to scout out talent for permanent employment with your company. If your intern is a Junior or Senior in college, you can make the offer of a position at a stated salary to start right after graduation. Many students look forward to such an offer and take internships very seriously, not only for a good grade, but for the possibility of a great reference or even a job.

Earlier in the book I touched on the possibility of diversifying your business. Interns can be a great help in these endeavors, and you will have a wider range of intern help to enlist. Your business may have nothing to do with computers, but if you decide to try diversifying into mail order over the Internet or gathering information on competitors, a computer-education intern would be perfect. Communications or marketing majors can be very helpful in dealing with your media reps for you.

Each intern will only be with you for one semester. If interning at your business is a positive learning experience for the student, you will have no trouble obtaining an intern every semester!

Co-op Advertising

Co-op advertising is an opportunity to get some help with the cost of advertising. Those of you in retail sales will find that some of your suppliers have commercials and co-op money available for advertising specific brands of merchandise. Many suppliers and franchise companies have programs in place which will pay up to 50 percent of your radio, television, outdoor, or print advertising. The amount you can expect to receive is based on a percentage of your orders, so look to your largest suppliers for help with co-op money, commercials, and print ads that are ready to go. For example, if the amount you have available from ABS brand is $1,000 based on your purchases from that company, you can buy up to $2,000 of advertising and be reimbursed for half of it.

Your media reps should be able to help you determine what amounts of co-op money you have available and the deadlines for using it. They will provide notarized scripts or copies of your ad required by co-op providers, and see that your invoices and other requirements are met on time. Co-op can be such a pain for some people they would rather lose out on the money than deal with it. However, ask your suppliers to make available their co-op guidelines — and then ask your reps to help make using it possible. Your media reps will probably have co-op books they can look through for participating manufacturers, listed alphabetically by brand names, to see what is available.

Once you determine what co-op dollars are available to you, write separate contracts for each product or brand and have your media reps write "co-op" and the appropriate brand name on all orders that apply. It will not only be proof that the advertising was indeed used for the correct brand (which will be part of the required paperwork), but if you are able to use co-op with more than one product, it will help you sort out paperwork at a later date. Always keep copies of co-op claims in a separate folder. Don't be put off if a supplier makes it sound complicated. Insist that all requirements are made clear at the onset. You can save a lot of money by persisting and your reps will gladly help because it means you are able to spend more money on advertising than you might be able to on your own.

Tip: Ask your radio, television, and print reps to alert you in advance of any upcoming special events or promotions that would tie in nicely with your business.

4

Radio

Radio is one of the easiest, fastest, and most powerful forms of advertising available as long as you know which stations in your market are best suited to your customers or clients. Even a medium-size market can have twenty or more radio stations from which to choose — each with a very specific audience to deliver.

Pay no attention to reports in your local newspapers or anywhere else that ranks your local radio stations using 12+ as a demographic. There is no one station that will appeal to everyone over the age of 12. To find the right station or stations to use for your business, you must be very specific as to age and gender groups. Use only the choices you made from demographic groups A and B in the beginning of this book — and you'll notice there is no 12+ choice — as your guide for your radio purchases.

Radio targets specific populations divided into groups by age and gender. That is precisely why you need to know who your customers are and which stations will deliver your message directly to them. Most stations have a primary and a secondary audience. However, the secondary group can be very small and not worth the price of advertising. While expert media buyers are able to spend not only hours, but days and weeks, dissecting primary and secondary audiences, it is in your best interest to simplify the options and choose stations according to their primary strengths. You will probably find two to four radio stations in your market with the right audience for your business. When several appropriate stations are available to you, one of them will have the lion's share of listeners and be the most expensive. There is nothing wrong with using the number 2 or even the number 3 station — if one exists — as long as the audience is made up of the demographic group you need. The rule of thumb is now and will always be that the larger the audience, the more expensive the station will be to use. Your Radio Worksheets will show you how to determine which stations will be useful to you.

Stations with different formats have audiences with different listening habits and you will need to incorporate this information into your buying decisions. Beautiful music, soft rock, talk radio, and country music have among the longest listening audiences while most other formats will have a younger listener who flips through stations in search of his/her favorite tune. When you use a station whose audience listens steadily for long periods of time, you can use fewer commercials than you can with a station catering to "channel surfers."

There will also be some "crossover" between stations with similar formats or even stations with different formats who cater to the same demographic groups. In other words, a Baby Boomer might listen to talk radio during the week and switch to a station broadcasting what is often known as "Golden Oldies" in the evenings and on weekends. They are crossing over from one station to another — therefore by advertising on just one of those stations, you are able to reach a portion of the second audience as well.

There are two tried and true ways of using radio successfully. "Tactical" advertising (that is, running a large number of commercials for a short period of time) or "strategic" or "maintenance" advertising (where you run a smaller schedule over a long period of time). While a schedule of 24 commercials per week for two weeks will get people into your store for a sale, a lower frequency schedule of 5–7 commercials per week will keep your business name and location out there as a reminder.

A store selling major appliances would use strategic advertising because major appliances don't break down every day. This type of store needs to create name awareness in the minds of the public so that when someone actually needs to buy a new washing machine he or she will think of that store as the first place to go. Telling the public that "This weekend you can save 25 percent on washing machines" works only for those people who need to buy one now — a very small percent of those who will need one eventually.

However, a store that wants to sell 500 plants on a given weekend will use tactical advertising, and buy a large amount of commercials in a 4 or 5 day period leading up to and including the sale weekend.

A popular way to make the most of a low frequency schedule is to purchase a *sponsorship*. Sponsorships are usually purchased on long term contracts, meaning at least 13 weeks, and are often purchased for 26 or 52 weeks. You purchase the right to have your business credited with bringing the news, sports, weather, traffic reports, etc., to the listening audience. This sponsoring is done with identifying *billboards,* or *Sponsor IDs*. Billboards explain, "This edition of the news is brought to you by the XYZ Paint Company." Along with the identifying billboard the paint company receives a :30 or :60 second commercial within a relatively close proximity of the actual report. You can usually purchase a sponsorship for 2–5 days per week, depending on your budget. Week in and week out, your company is credited with your chosen report(s) and the audience gets used to hearing your name.

Commercials accompanying a news, weather, traffic or sports report receive more attention than commercials plugged into musical sequences. Because the audience is listening for specific information and is paying close attention to these reports, it is said to be in a *listening mode*. Along the same lines, it can be argued that commercials placed in talk radio shows are heard more readily. Listeners pay attention to large segments of this format because they are interested in the subject matter or enjoy listening to a popular show host. They are also in a listening mode.

The best of all possible worlds is to be able to afford a low frequency 52 week sponsorship and also be able to add higher frequency schedules several times a year for sales or special events.

Most stations offer discounts for long term, *consecutive week* contracts. Usually 5% for a 26 week contract and 10 percent for a 52 week contract. If you have received a discount for making a long term commitment, you can insist on being given the same discount for any additional schedules you place during the life of the contract. Not only are discounts offered for long term contracts, but you will receive a price break for *high frequency* schedules. For example, you will pay less per commercial (spot) when you run 18 of them in one week then you would pay per spot for a 12X per week schedule. And you will pay less per spot for 24X per week than you will for 18X.

Generally, the 24X per week schedule is the most you would ever need to purchase in one week on any one station. At that point, added frequency can inch you toward the point of diminishing return where you find yourself spending money unnecessarily — in short — overkill. Radio Worksheet #2 will show you samples of 12X, 18X, and 24X schedules for building traffic to your business during the early part of the week, mid-week, on weekends, or all week long.

If you have the budget to run 24 commercials each week — do it. Don't hold back to see what will happen if you only run 12 commercials. As you've always heard with buying real estate, the #1 consideration is location, location, location. The same thing applies when buying radio, but add frequency, frequency, frequency to the saying. Always run as many commercials as you can afford and never run more than you can afford.

Radio rate sheets are called "wish lists" largely because the printed rates are the ones the stations wish they could get. Remember, the rule of thumb is that the stations with the largest audiences are the stations with the highest rates. When a station rep comes to you with a sales pitch of "buy one commercial, get one commercial free," it means that they have a lot of unsold inventory there — maybe because it's the first quarter when all stations can use business — or maybe it's because the station has no audience to speak of and can be generous in hopes of getting your business.

In reality, you can negotiate a lower rate than the ones shown on any rate sheet. During first and third quarters when advertising is always down, you can negotiate a great annual contract and enjoy the lower rates all year long.

Instead of charging more for a :60 second spot than a :30 as they did for years, radio stations now sell "units" of advertising and charge the same rate for a :30 or a :60 second spot. They define units as the number of different messages a listener hears in any one commercial break. A two-minute break can hold four :30 second spots, two :60 second spots, or a combination of the two. A listener perceives the four :30 second spots as taking longer than the two :60 second spots (even though the same number of seconds is used) because he hears 4 different messages instead of two. This effort to have the listeners perceive as few commercials as possible, and knowing that most advertisers would choose :60s over :30s, was the biggest reason to switch to unit pricing. Whichever length of commercial you decide to use, ask your reps for the best possible rate. Then when you call to actually place an order, ask if they can do even better. Don't be afraid to let your reps know you are calling around to get the best deal possible.

Your radio salesperson may represent two or more stations — combinations of AM and FM stations owned by the same company — very often with studios and offices in the same building. You can take advantage of a lower "combo rate" if you are willing to buy time on two or more of these stations instead of just one. Be sure any stations you combine meet your demographic requirements. At this time there are no regulations on how many stations can be owned by one company, but you will usually not find a radio salesperson representing more than two of the stations at a time.

Getting Help with Copy Writing and Production

Copy writing: Unless you're prolific and can put together a radio script timed to exactly :30 or :60 seconds, or have lots of time to spend laboring over a commercial message, look to your radio rep(s) with whom you do business to write the scripts for you.

If you are new to radio and are not sure of the talent available, have a script prepared at each of the stations you will be using and ask for a cassette from each to listen to. Choose the one you like the best and ask for one copy, or "dub" of the commercial for each of the other stations. There will be a talent fee for the person voicing the commercial and a small charge for each copy. If you are using only one station there should be no production fee or talent fee. Those charges usually only kick in when you take the talent — in the form of a commercial voice — from one station and use it on another. The copy writing is free of charge and is done by either your sales rep or an actual copy writer employed by the station.

The name and location of your business should be mentioned at least twice in a :30 second ad and 3 times in a :60 second ad. If you are having a sale, give price and item, a percent off amount, or a specific brand being sold at a discounted price. You will find there is not much room in :30 seconds for cute comments, sound effects, or even for a two-voice script. Save those extras for your :60 second scripts.

If you have lots of information to cover, either use one :60 second script or two :30 second commercials — splitting the information between the two and rotating the two ads throughout your schedule. When rotating two commercials, be sure that the opening, the voice, the music, and the general feeling of the ads are the same so your audience will hear all of the information in both ads without being distracted by two completely different sounding commercials.

Don't squeeze too much into your radio script. Stay focused on material that has the best chance of motivating people to come in or call. Listen to national commercials on your radio. A company promoting its shampoo will not say "And we also sell toothpaste" at the end.

Simply saying that you exist and listing items you sell or services you render will not do it. Concentrate on specific information that makes it important and beneficial for people to come to your store or office instead of one of your competitors. Make each ad a call to action! If you don't make that case — if there is no motivation for them to come to your location instead of your competitor, you will be one of the people who say, "I tried radio and it doesn't work."

Perhaps you will grow to the point of being able to run "image" commercials, which sort of float around keeping your name in front of the public for no specific reason other than to remind them of your existence. Image commercials tend to relay the flavor or essence of your business to the listener rather then being motivational in nature.

Using a word processor, typewriter, or a computer with an 11 point or comparable size font, use the following eight-line sheet for a standard :30 second script. A :60 second commercial equals approximately 16 typed lines. Do not use

:30 Second Script / Title _____ **Date** _____

1) CHECK OUT THE INVENTORY CLEARANCE SALE GOING ON TODAY THROUGH

2) SUNDAY AT <u>SHARP WINDOW</u>, CENTRAL NEW YORK'S LARGEST WINDOW AND

3) WINDOW TREATMENT STORE. ALL DRAPERIES, CURTAINS, MINI BLINDS, AND

4) IN-STOCK STAINED GLASS INSERTS ARE MARKED AT **FIFTY PERCENT** OFF

5) ALREADY DISCOUNTED PRICES! ALL ACCESSORIES, DECORATIVE CURTAIN

6) RODS, TIE-BACKS, AND VALANCES NOW **SIXTY PERCENT** OFF! SHOP EARLY

7) FOR BEST SELECTION WHILE SUPPLIES LAST! SHOP THIS MONUMENTAL SALE

8) NOW THROUGH SUNDAY AT <u>SHARP WINDOW</u>, FIFTH STREET IN ROCHESTER.

Special instructions: _____

_____

_____

_____

_____

_____

_____

:60 Second Script / Title _____ **Date** _____

1) CHECK OUT THE INVENTORY CLEARANCE SALE GOING ON TODAY THROUGH

2) SUNDAY AT <u>SHARP WINDOW</u>, CENTRAL NEW YORK'S LARGEST WINDOW AND

3) WINDOW TREATMENT STORE. ALL DRAPERIES, CURTAINS, MINI BLINDS, AND

4) IN-STOCK STAINED GLASS INSERTS ARE MARKED AT **FIFTY PERCENT** OFF

5) ALREADY DISCOUNTED PRICES! ALL ACCESSORIES, DECORATIVE WOOD

6) AND METAL CURTAIN RODS, TIE-BACKS, AND VALANCES ARE NOW PRICED

7) AT **SIXTY PERCENT** OFF! THIS IS THE _LARGEST_ SALE YOU WILL FIND ALL

8) YEAR AT <u>SHARP WINDOW</u>, SO SHOP EARLY FOR THE BEST SELECTION! THE

9) WINDOW TREATMENT YOU'VE BEEN DREAMING OF IS ON SALE NOW! DON'T

10) MISS THIS OPPORTUNITY TO BUY THE VERY BEST AT THE LOWEST PRICES

11) OF THE YEAR. AND DURING THIS INVENTORY CLEARANCE SALE,

12) <u>SHARP WINDOW</u> HAS REDUCED THE PRICE OF THOUSANDS OF ROLLS OF

13) IN-STOCK CUSTOM DRAPERY FABRIC TO JUST _ONE DOLLAR A YARD_ — WHILE

14) SUPPLIES LAST! SHOP THIS MONUMENTAL SALE NOW THROUGH SUNDAY

15) AT <u>SHARP WINDOW</u>, TEN-FIFTY THREE FIFTH STREET IN ROCHESTER, NEXT

16) TO CHARLIE'S TROPHY SHOP. OR CALL 555-9999 FOR MORE INFORMATION!

Special instructions: _____

_____

_____

abbreviations, numerals, or substitute "&" for "and." All words take the same amount of time to say no matter how you write them. So, for an accurately timed script, spell out all the words. Use all caps for easier reading. Spell difficult-to-pronounce words phonetically. Lines are double-spaced to allow changes or notes by the person voicing the spot. Copy the blank form onto your business letterhead.

Production: Once you have tried the production at a few stations, as suggested in the copy writing section, and you feel comfortable with the quality of any one particular station, use that production facility for all your work. Obviously, if your schedule does not include that station for a particular schedule, your production will need to be done at one of the stations you will be using.

Keep in mind that people listening to radio are usually doing something else at the same time — driving, working in the home or at the office, or exercising, so they don't necessarily hear every word in a commercial. If you can manage the cost of having one commercial produced (including talent fee and the cost of copies to give to other stations you are using), it's a plus if all commercials sound the same on all stations. However, if you are using more than one station and you would like to avoid paying production fees, give your finalized script to each station and let them produce their own versions at no cost to you. The material will be the same — the delivery will end up being very different unless you give instructions that will standardize the spots.

Request a female or male voice on all spots, the same music, and the kind of energy you want put into the voice ("energetic read" or "laid back, casual read"). This way, each audience will hear the same words and receive the same message at little or no cost to you. While it may be more appealing to have the same exact commercial on all stations, new businesses do not always have funds to pay for production. And in that case it is smarter to put whatever money you do have into the frequency of the schedule and run a basic but informative ad.

Always ask to hear the final product before it airs. The station(s) will be happy to play it for you over the phone or provide a cassette. Feel free to ask that the voice be more upbeat or that the music be changed to suit you. Listen to it again after the changes have been made.

Once your commercial has been produced, ask your rep to give you the master reel if you think you might use it again in the future. Radio stations will store tapes, but on a rare occasion one can be misplaced or taped over. If your ad has the potential to be used again, keep it in a cool, dry place where you can find it in a hurry. Label the box with the date and title and put a copy of the typed script in the box so you can review it quickly to see if prices or brands, etc. are still appropriate when you go to use it again.

Franchise operators will often have access to canned radio commercials through their advertising support system. A single phone call can put a professionally produced commercial in your hands within a day or two. Usually there will be a blank space at the end of these commercials for "tagging" with your local address, phone number or sale details.

Those of you in retail sales may find that distributors of brand name merchandise also have professionally produced radio commercials ready to go and often co-op advertising assistance is available in the forms of not only produced commercials but also money.

Promotions and Trade Advertising: Promotions and trade advertising are two popular forms of advertising designed to bring extra impact to a special event. They often go hand-in-hand, therefore they will be discussed together. A promotion is a happening, over and above usual advertising. For example, if a book store runs a sale of 20 percent off everything in the store, it's normal advertising. If the store is offering 20 percent off a new bestseller, has the author on the premises to sign copies, and perhaps even runs a contest to have dinner with the author — it's a promotion.

You may engage in a promotion with one station or with several. Your budget will have a lot to do with the decision. Always choose a station or stations able to provide you with the correct audience(s). If you have an idea for a promotion, ask your rep(s) to consider participating in the special event. Outline the details, specify the budget you are prepared to expend, and ask what they can offer in the way of free promotional announcements, appearances by one or more of their personalities, or with remotes (having one of the personalities host part of a broadcast from your location). Your budget, the right station(s), and the excitement you create with your advertising will pretty much determine the success or failure of your promotion.

It needs to be mentioned here that Mother Nature has been known to foil the most carefully planned event. If you're going to be outside or if people need to travel any distance to take part, the weather can be a maker or a breaker. Depending on your location and the time of year, you may lose the day to excessive heat, humidity, rain, blizzards, wind storms, or hazardous road conditions.

You'll find that radio stations will frequently come to you looking for participants in a promotional event they have cooked up. They are often in need of prizes for on-air contests such as get-away vacations, automobiles, tickets to concerts or plays, gift certificates, and general merchandise. They are also often in need of goods and/or services for themselves such as printing, landscaping, decorating, office furniture, vehicle maintenance, computers, copiers, janitorial services and more. And they will be anxious to trade advertising for them.

Many times you can negotiate what is known as a half cash/half trade agreement with a station allowing that 50 percent of the advertising is paid in cash and the other 50 percent is taken in merchandise or services from your business.

When participating in trade advertising, use your retail price or full service hourly rate to figure the dollar amount and always think of it as cash. Most stations will want you to sign a contract stating that the trade portion of your advertising is pre-emptable. That is, if enough paying customers are available to buy the air space promised to you, they will bump your trade ad in favor of the cash customer and run your ad when space again becomes available. Always try to negotiate that pre-empt clause from the contract. You will have the most luck with this in the first and third quarters when demand for air time is not so high.

The single most important consideration in deciding to participate in trade advertising is whether the station can provide you with the audience you need. If a station cannot deliver the audience you need, do not participate no matter how great it sounds! Trade can be tempting because not all of the advertising is paid in cash. But advertising on a station you would not otherwise use is wasting the value of the merchandise you give away or the services you provide. Even when making a cash/trade deal with one of your appropriate stations, you must consider the cost of your merchandise or service... and think of it as cash. And always, always, always put end dates on every gift certificate, coupon, or offer. If you don't, you will be honoring them as long as they keep appearing ... years after the offer was over.

When participating in a trade agreement, ask for promotional announcements to accompany your advertising schedule. This means that every time the upcoming event is promoted, your business will be mentioned as a provider of the prize(s). Most promotions are heavily scheduled through the weeks preceding the event and these promotional mentions mean your business name will be heard over and over again. Trade and promotion are creative ways of adding impact to your advertising projects. Tell your sales people you are interested and to keep you in mind when opportunities arise.

Schedule frequency: Correct radio schedule frequencies can be complicated to determine. For those of you who would like to take the time to gather, dissect, and calculate extensive amounts of Arbitron information, here are some definitions and equations you can use. Don't feel badly if you don't want to do this — you don't really need to. Your completed radio worksheets will give you all the information you need to conduct an accurate, targeted, no-nonsense advertising program. Don't forget that with four Arbitron books per year, these calculations need to be done each time. However, perusing the following equations will show you why advertising is a full-time job for those who love it. You will also see how valuable the worksheets in this book are and how much time and money they save you when it's time to promote your business.

Average Quarter-Hour Persons: (AQH) The average number of people listening to one station for at least 5 minutes out of a given 15 minute period. You can get these numbers from your rep(s).

Average Quarter-Hour Rating: The average AQH estimate shown as a percent of the sampled population. You can ask your sales rep for this figure in the MSA (Metro Survey Area) or the TSA (Total Survey Area). Both MSA and TSA were defined with the sample coverage maps on pages 52 and 54. The math equation you use to determine this figure is:

$$\frac{\text{AQH Persons}}{\text{Population}} \quad x \quad 100 \quad = \quad \text{AQH rating, or percent}$$

Cume Persons: The total number of different people who listen to one radio station for a minimum of 5 minutes during any one daypart. (Four dayparts being divided into morning, midday, afternoon and evening.)

Cume Rating: The total number of different people (Cume persons) shown as a percent of the estimated population of a specific demographic group.

$$\frac{\text{Cume Persons}}{\text{Population}} \quad x \quad 100 \quad = \quad \text{Cume rating (\%)}$$

Rating: The audience shown as a percent of the total population.

$$\frac{\text{Listeners}}{\text{Population}} \quad x \quad 100 \quad = \quad \text{Rating (\%)}$$

Share: The percent of all people listening to radio in general in the MSA who are tuned in to one particular station.

$$\frac{\text{AQH Persons of One Station}}{\text{AQH persons of all stations}} \quad x \quad 100 \quad = \quad \text{Share (\%)}$$

Gross Impressions (GIs): The total audience of AQH persons available for the total # of commercials in any given schedule.

AQH persons x number of commercials in a given schedule = GIs

Gross Rating Points (GRPs): The total of all rating points gained for a given schedule.

AQH rating x number of commercials in a given schedule = GRPs

Cost Per Rating Point: The cost of reaching the AQH listening audience equal to 1 % of the population in any one demographic group. This can be calculated in two ways:

$$\frac{\textbf{Cost of Schedule}}{\text{GRP}} = \text{Cost per rating point} \qquad \frac{\textbf{Average Cost Per Spot}}{\text{AQH rating}} = \text{Cost per rating point}$$

Cost per thousand (CPM): The price of delivering 1,000 gross impressions. This can also be calculated in two ways.

$$\frac{\textbf{Price of Schedule}}{\text{Gross impressions x 1,000}} = \text{CPM} \qquad \frac{\textbf{Spot Cost}}{\text{AQH persons x 1,000}} = \text{CPM}$$

Frequency: The average number of times a person has the opportunity to hear a radio schedule.

$$\frac{\textbf{Gross Impressions}}{\text{Net reach}} = \text{Frequency}$$

You can only get the numbers you need for these equations from a radio rep whose station subscribes to Arbitron. Those who do not subscribe are not allowed under any circumstances to use or supply specific Arbitron numbers to clients or to use Arbitron numbers in making a pitch for their station or against another station. Most radio stations do subscribe and will be happy to furnish you with whatever numbers you need to do the math. Your radio account executive(s) will be happy to go through the steps with you.

About Worksheet #1

Worksheet #1 provides a general overview of a radio station — current information regarding a station's audience, prices, and available sponsorships. You should have this information on all stations that meet your demographic requirements. Have this worksheet (as well as radio worksheets #2 and #3) filled out by all radio sales reps who call on you. Throw away any sets that come back to you with Sections A & B not matching the same sections you filled out on page 4. Keep the ones that have circled the same choices under groups A and B for both your primary and secondary audiences for future use.

Using X = 1 commercial, you can see how a schedule of 12 commercials, 18 commercials, or 24 commercials per week would be placed both during the week and on weekends.

Worksheet #1

Radio

HAVE YOUR REP FILL OUT AND RETURN THIS SHEET.

Radio Station Information

Call Letters ___WAZQ___   Dial Position ___106.9___

Rep's Name: ___John Doe___   Phone Number: ___555-5500 Fax 555-5501___

Format: ___Country___

Demographic Strength: Sales Rep: Circle the choices from Groups A and B that best describe your station's primary strength.

Group A (age)	Group B (sex)
18–34	(Female)
18–49	Male
(25–54)	Adults (both male and female)
50+	

Cost per week based on frequency of 12X, 18X, 24X Monday – Friday 5:30A – 10 P.

12X per week $ __1,170.00__   (3X 5:30a – 10a, 3X 10a – 3p, 3X 3p –7p, 3X 7p – 10p)
18X per week $ __1,710.00__   (4X 5:30a – 10a, 5X 10a – 3p, 5X 3p –7p, 4X 7p – 10p)
24X per week $ __2,208.00__   (6X 5:30a – 10a, 6X 10a – 3p, 6X 3p –7p, 6X 7p – 10p)

Cost per week based on weekends (Friday –Sunday) 10A –10P.

12X per week $ __1,080.00__   (4X 10a – 3p, 4X 3p –7p, 4X 7p – 10p)
18X per week $ __1,575.00__   (6X 10a – 3p, 6X 3p –7p, 6X 7p – 10p)
24X per week $ __2,040.00__   (8X 10a – 3p, 8X 3p –7p, 8X 7p – 10p)

SPONSORSHIP AVAILABLE

Type of Sponsorship	Times per Week	Price per Week	Audience	
News	2X (T, Th)	$ __250.00__	__35-54__	(age)
Billboards	3X (M, W, F)	$ __375.00__		
(are)/are not included	5X (M – F)	$ __625.00__	__F__	(sex)
Weather	2X (T, Th)	$ __300.00__	__25-54__	(age)
Billboards	3X (M, W, F)	$ __450.00__		
are/are not included	5X (M – F)	$ __750.00__	__F__	(sex)
Sports	2X (T, Th)	$ __250.00__	__25-45__	(age)
Billboards	3X (M, W, F)	$ __375.00__		
are/are not included	5X (M – F)	$ __625.00__	__F__	(sex)
Air Traffic	2X (T, Th)	$ __300.00__	__25-54__	(age)
Billboards	3X (M, W, F)	$ __450.00__		
are/are not included	5X (M – F)	$ __750.00__	__F__	(sex)

For example, using the first schedule shown on Worksheet #1 of 12 commercials (spots) per week, airing Monday through Friday, the commercials would be placed as follows:

(3X) 5:30 AM – 10 AM, (3X) 10 AM – 3 PM,
(3X) 3 PM – 7 PM, (3X) 7 PM – 10 PM

This means that during the 5 day period , three of your commercials will run between 5:30 AM and 10 AM (morning drive), three will run between 10 AM and 3 PM (mid-day), three will run between 3 PM and 7 PM (afternoon drive), and three will run in the evening between 7 PM and 10 PM. You can tell your rep that you would like a 6 AM start and a 9 PM cut off (depending on what time your business or event closes at night) on any schedules that run all day. Feel free to mold the hours to where you really want them.

An all-day schedule is called a TAP plan and is designed to run throughout all day-parts for a slightly lower rate. TAP stands for Total Audience Plan because it reaches listeners morning, noon, and night — therefore giving your message a chance to be heard by all of the different people who listen to that station during every part of the day. At most stations "morning drive" Monday through Friday is the most expensive, "afternoon drive" is next, "mid-day" is next and "evening" is the least expensive. Weekends are usually less than weekdays and you can pay next to nothing to advertise overnight between midnight and 5 AM, but your audience is severely reduced. However, if you are in an area where factories and hospitals require a lot of shift work, you may actually see a little response from overnight.

Since most radio stations now sell "units" rather than :30 or :60 second spots, your rep will fill in the rates on Worksheet #1 with unit prices. Units are defined as the number of different messages a listener hears in any commercial break. In other words, a commercial break of 3 minutes can hold six :30 second spots, or three :60 second spots. A listener will perceive the three :60 second spots as "only" three commercials while the same listener might become annoyed at listening to six different :30 second spots — even though the same amount of commercial time has elapsed.

Because of this leaning toward selling units, you are able to purchase a :60 second spot for the same price as a :30 second spot. You may ask why anyone would choose a :30 when they can have a :60 for the same price? National chains, manufacturers with co-op spots, franchise advertising support, etc. often produce their spots in :30 second format. Also, many stations attach :30 second spots to their sponsorship packages of news, sports, weather, or traffic.

While some people in radio sales are of the opinion that :60 seconds worth of any commercial message is boring to the listening audience, you should make that determination yourself. When I am developing a commercial, I will always use :60 seconds if the prices are the same. I like having more time to repeat important facts and dates, being more creative with copy and hammering away at the business name and location. Getting copy writing help from creative reps will help keep your material interesting for the listeners. It might be a good idea to re-read the section on copy writing and production before you start making your list of ideas for your radio rep(s).

When the cost for :30 second and :60 second spots is not the same, it is important to consider the number of commercials you can purchase with your budget. The frequency with which your message is heard is paramount to the success of your radio advertising. If buying eight :60 second spots cost the same as buying fourteen :30 second spots, go with the higher frequency. It is always better to use more (even though shorter in length) commercials to give the audience a greater opportunity to hear your message. Remember — it's not only location, location, location, but also frequency, frequency, frequency!

Tip: Famous radio and television personalities like Bruce Williams and Sally Jesse Raphael can be contacted by their sponsoring stations for voice-over work.

About Worksheet #2

When do you need to bolster business? While some businesses such as garden shops and theme parks need advertising to build weekend traffic, diet companies often like to advertise on Mondays because most people start diets on that day. Many restaurants want to build mid-week lunch business while others want to advertise all during the week.

Whether you need to increase business during the early portion of the week, mid-week, on the weekends, or business in general all week long, there are samples of properly placed schedules shown on Worksheet #2.

These examples of radio schedules with different frequencies, are designed to bolster your business at various times of the week. Early week, meaning Monday and Tuesday, and weekends, are usually the least expensive days to advertise. And because those days are less commercially crowded, your ads might have a better chance of being heard.

Each section of this schedule sheet represents a 12X schedule, an 18X schedule, and a 24X schedule, which are all classic frequencies. A schedule of 12

Worksheet #2

Radio

X = One Commercial   Station: WAZQ

Sample General Weekday Schedules

12X	M	T	W	Th	F
6–10A	X		X		X
10–3P		X	X	X	
3–7P	X		X		X
7–10P		X	X	X	

Cost $ 1,170.00

18X	M	T	W	Th	F
6–10A	X		X	X	X
10–3P	X	X	X	X	X
3–7P	X	X	X	X	X
7–10P	X	X	X	X	

Cost $ 1,710.00

24X	M	T	W	Th	F
6–10A	XX	X	X	X	X
10–3P	X	X	XX	X	X
3–7P	X	XX	X	X	X
7–10P	X	X	X	XX	X

Cost $ 2,208.00

Sample Schedules for Early Mid-Week Business

12X	M	T	W
6–10A	X	X	X
10–3P	XX	X	X
3–7P	X	XX	
7–10P	X	X	

Cost $ 1,170.00

18X	M	T	W
6–10A	XX	X	XX
10–3P	XX	XX	XX
3–7P	XX	X	
7–10P	XX	XX	

Cost $ 1,710.00

24X	M	T	W
6–10A	XXX	XX	XX
10–3P	XX	XXX	XX
3–7P	XXX	XX	
7–10P	XX	XXX	

Cost $ 2,208.00

Sample Schedules for Late Week and Weekend Business

12X	M	T	W	Th	F	Sat
6–10A			X	X	X	
10–3P				X	X	X
3–7P				X	X	X
7–10P			X	X	X	

Cost $ 1,080.00

18X	M	T	W	Th	F	Sat
6–10A				X	X	XX
10–3P				XX	X	XX
3–7P				X	XX	XX
7–10P				X	XX	X

Cost $ 1,575.00

24X	M	T	W	Th	F	Sat
6–10A			X	XX	XX	X
10–3P			X	X	XX	XX
3–7P			X	XX	XX	X
7–10P			X	XX	XX	X

Cost $ 2,040.00

Sample Schedules for Weekend Business

12X	F	Sat	Sun
6–10A			
10–3P		XX	XX
3–7P	XX	XX	
7–10P	XX	XX	

Cost $ 1,080.00

18X	F	Sat	Sun
6–10A			
10–3P		XXX	XXX
3–7P	XXX	XXX	
7–10P	XXX	XXX	

Cost $ 1,575.00

24X	F	Sat	Sun
6–10A			
10–3P		XXXX	XXXX
3–7P	XXXX	XXXX	
7–10P	XXXX	XXXX	

Cost $ 2,040.00

If you are not open Sunday or your event ends on Saturday, move Sunday spots back into commercials per week, per station, is the lowest frequency you should ever use, 18X per week on any one station is a decent frequency, and 24X is standard. Use the highest frequency your budget will allow. ThirtyX to 40X per week, per radio station is a great frequency for a sale. Skimping is a great way to undermine your advertising success.

While sponsorships of news, sports, traffic or weather are best for low frequency, long-term maintenance, and image advertising, the examples shown on the sample schedule sheet are for higher frequency, shorter term schedules geared for sales, special events, and normal weekly advertising. This worksheet will make it very easy to find a schedule at a glance and have it placed with just a phone call to your rep. Ask your reps to give you current costs for each of the schedules every business quarter.

> **Tip: Avoid dejá-moo**, which means "I've heard that bull before." Keep phrases like "… and much, much, more!" out of your copy. Put effort into making your commercials sound refreshing — not the same old bull.

Worksheet # 3

Four times a year, radio stations are ranked by the survey company Arbitron and they are willing to pay large sums of money to secure the resulting information. When touting the benefits of a radio station, your sales reps may refer to the "numbers in the last book." They are referring to the station's position compared to all of the other radio stations in the same market as determined by the latest survey information. Four surveys a year result in four "books" a year — each book indicating the rise or fall of each station's ranking as compared to the previous book. The surveys follow the seasons, so there will be a summer book, a fall book, a winter book, and a spring book each year.

In any one book there exists many different kinds of information. Determining Reach and Frequency is the process of answering two basic questions: **Reach** equals how many *different* people hear your commercial at least one time during your schedule and **Frequency** equals how many times each unduplicated person hear the spot. Current wisdom says the listener needs to hear the spot 2.5 times before he will act on it. The average time spent listening (does the station's format hold the audience for long periods of time or is it a station with "channel surfers"?) determines to some extent how many commercials you need to run on any single station to achieve that magic 2.5 number. Therefore the number of spots you run is just as important as choosing the correct station in the first place. Your radio sales reps can help you determine how many commercials you need to run to be sure your schedule has the best chance of succeeding.

Worksheet #3

Radio Demographic Rankings

Station: __WAZQ__   Date: __9/6/98__

Circle the same choices below from Groups A and B as you did in Chapter 1. Have your radio rep(s) fill out only the sections that match those selections. This worksheet, when completed by your reps, will indicate how the top four stations reaching your desired audience(s) compare to each other. The information will be excerpted from research companies such as Arbitron and Neilsen and represents the most accurate data available.

Group A (age)	Group B (sex)
18–34	(Female)
18–49	Male
(25–54)	Adults (both male and female)
50+	

Source: __Arbitron - Summer '98__   Note to Rep: Please use average persons (00)
Market: Total Survey Area

Monday – Friday 5:30 AM to 10 PM

Women 18–34	Men 18–34	Adults 18–34
1. _____	_____	_____
2. _____	_____	_____
3. _____	_____	_____
4. _____	_____	_____

Women 18–49	Men 18–49	Adults 18–49
1. _____	_____	_____
2. _____	_____	_____
3. _____	_____	_____
4. _____	_____	_____

(Women 25–54)	Men 25–54	Adults 25–54
1. WNTA	_____	_____
2. WAZQ	_____	_____
3. WWWX	_____	_____
4. WKNZ	_____	_____

Women 50+	Men 50+	Adults 50+
1. _____	_____	_____
2. _____	_____	_____
3. _____	_____	_____
4. _____	_____	_____

Worksheet #3 # Radio Demographic Rankings, continued

Saturday – Sunday 9 AM to Midnight

Women 18–34	Men 18–34	Adults 18–34
1.		
2.		
3.		
4.		

Women 18–49	Men 18–49	Adults 18–49
1.		
2.		
3.		
4.		

Women 25–54	Men 25–54	Adults 25–54
1. WAZQ		
2. WWWX		
3. WNTA		
4. WKNZ		

Women 50+	Men 50+	Adults 50+
1.		
2.		
3.		
4.		

Notes: Station is interested in 1/2 cash, 1/2 trade.

Submitted by: John Doe   WAZQ   9/6/98

         Name of Salesperson   Station   Date

Directions on Worksheet #3 instruct your salesperson to pull data from Arbitron using the Total Survey Area (TSA) which will include representative audiences in the widest range of a station's signal. Ask each rep for a *coverage map* and determine for yourself if you want numbers from their TSA or from the Metro Survey Area (MSA) the latter of which is the smaller, more localized area. Most coverage maps will have two circles — one within the other. The larger circle represents the TSA and the smaller circle represents the MSA.

The rep of a small radio station might come to you and say, "Why pay higher rates to reach people who live so far away when my station's audience, although smaller, is 100 percent local?" While this may sound perfectly logical, if you compare the actual numbers of people listening in the MSA of both stations, you will probably find that the larger station has thousands more listeners locally even though it has a strong enough signal to also reach people farther away.

Before handing out this two-paged worksheet, **go through both pages and circle only the headings that coincide with the choices you made from Groups A & B in the Customer Information Section.** This worksheet will provide you with a list of the top 4 stations catering to the audience you need. Keep the appropriate ones for future use. Because there are four books each year, have the sheets updated for each book to keep you current.

Keep in mind that Arbitron ratings are about audience *estimates*. Many advertisers like to look at the trends over 3 or 4 consecutive books. Every now and then an aberrant book turns up and a station with low ratings suddenly leaps to new heights without having changed its format, its personalities ... in other words, without any apparent reason. At the same time it is possible for the opposite to happen when a strong station takes a dive. It is wise to wait until the *next* book comes out to see if the ratings stay the same or show more normal results. Usually, a drastic rise or fall of any one station which has had no major change is due to a "bad book" in which a true reading was not able to be obtained.

Your salespeople may also invoke audience *psychographic* data along with demographic data as another point of influence. While demographics measure the age and gender of population segments, psychographics measure education, wealth, habits, hobbies, etc. in an attempt to show how smart, wealthy and/or active any given target group may be. It may be skating on relatively thin ice to bank too much on this kind of information. In today's society there exists so much paranoia, that I do not believe a high enough percent of these surveys are returned with totally accurate responses. I think many people consciously or unconsciously feel that there will be an identifying feature to any survey they participate in and that someone, somehow, somewhere, will be able to link them to the information they provide. Very few people today will admit that they did not finish high school and are prone to responding to a higher level of education then may be the actual case. Human nature tends to nudge some into claiming to make more money than they really do, being more active and interesting than they really are, and even being younger with more exciting hobbies.

There are thousands of lists bought and sold every day with the names of people who attend seminars, rent cars, buy carpeting, wear glasses, and subscribe to magazines. These kinds of lists are reliable because they come from businesses already catering to groups with specific interests. But the data solicited from individuals or from individual households requiring personal information may not be as trustworthy. In any case, you will most likely be given more demographic than psychographic information to digest and demographic is the safer of the two.

When a station changes to a new format, you will need to have your worksheets updated to reflect its new expected audience. A new format usually needs time to settle into the community and allow its new audience to take root.

If you have a contract with a radio station and that station changes its format, you not only have the ability to cancel your contract immediately, but you *should* do so immediately. Even if the new format is expected to have the same demographic profile as the old one, it will take time for people to get used to it and decide if they want to keep listening there or move on to another station. Your rep(s) should notify you as soon as any major change is made — even before the change occurs if possible. If you keep your completed worksheets as suggested, you can quickly call a rep from another appropriate station and continue your advertising.

Tip: Request a "client copy" of all radio spots on a cassette and all television spots on VHS for yourself *at the time of production.* You may be charged a small fee or nothing at all for this service and you will then have the ability to review your ads anytime you wish.

Tip: If your business rents, services, washes, repairs, or has anything else to do with vehicles, check the radio in every car, van, or truck, to see what station your customer was listening to. Keep a list and you'll soon see which stations you can use effectively.

Tip: Request a minimum of 15 minutes separation time between your radio and television spots and those being run by your competitors.

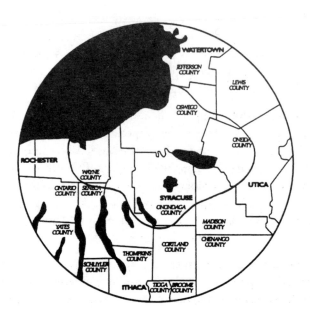

By looking at this coverage map, you can determine if this radio station will be beneficial for your location(s). The large outside circle shows the outer reaches of this station's signal or TSA (Total Survey Area) and the smaller inside circle indicates the more local MSA (Metro Survey Area) reach of the station's signal.

There are two basic types of commercials — image and motivational. An image commercial contains generic information about a business, product, or service. It's a commercial you can use as long as the information remains relevant and there are no date-specific sales or special events, no outdated discounts mentioned in the ad — no special reason for the reader, listener, or viewer, to respond in a timely fashion. An image commercial gives an overall picture and perception of your business, mentions a variety of products or services available, gives your location(s) and phone number(s), and perhaps your business hours. The audience is being told what you do, or what you have there that might interest them either today, tomorrow, or next year. This is an image message in the strictest form.

There is also an "in-between" commercial message that does not deal with special sales or time-sensitive promotions, but does mention regular, everyday prices. This too can be considered an image commercial.

The motivational commercial provides time-sensitive information on sales, grand openings, special events, clearances, liquidation sales, etc. It is meant to create a sense of urgency in the mind of your customers — to coax them into action. This type of script is written more with hype — that is, lots of excitement. Request that the person reading your script use an "energetic read" and ask for some appropriate "upbeat" music for the background.

While radio, television, and some forms of print make it easy to change a commercial from image to motivational, other forms of advertising do not. The copy you use in your outdoor and transit advertising stays put for at least a month, so while image advertising here works well, you will read in the Outdoor section of this book how to turn image into motivational advertising on billboards. While you can change your newspaper and radio copy on a daily or weekly basis, it's too expensive to produce a number of different television ads. Production costs are covered in detail in the various chapters of this book.

Developing several sales or promotions that you continue to run on an annual basis gives you the ability to produce one ad for each specific sale as well as a basic generic ad that you can use for more than one year. A shoe store might replace its generic ad in August for a "Back-to-School" sale, in November for a "Winter Boot" sale, and in June for a "Sneaker and Sandals" sale. These promotions take time to become recognized as annual events, but your customers will eventually get used to the sales and look for them.

In the Television Section of this book, it is suggested that a generic :30 second commercial with a :10 second tag (blank space) at the end of the spot is a great way to turn a generic spot into a motivational spot. Change only the audio (voice) section of the last :10 seconds of the commercial to reflect the current sale or promotion. Always have the production person save the original generic spot in its entirety so you can go back to it again without generating additional production cost.

Here are samples of a "strict" :30 second image script, a "regular" :30 second image script, and a :30 second motivational script for a restaurant. The "strict" image copy lets the audience know where the restaurant is and what they can generally expect to find there. It creates a homey, cozy atmosphere and hopefully makes people hungry. The second piece of image copy does the same thing but adds in an everyday price for breakfast to sweeten the message a little. The motivational copy gives the audience a reason to go to the restaurant for breakfast during a particular time period.

:30 Second/"Strict" Image Message

WHEN YOU'RE NOT QUITE AWAKE, AND NOT QUITE READY TO DRIVE TO WORK, STOP AT MAGGIE'S ON ROUTE 11 IN NORTH SYRACUSE FOR A HOMESTYLE BREAKFAST — COOKED JUST THE WAY YOU LIKE IT. MAGGIE'S ALSO HAS A BREAKFAST BAR FIT FOR A KING INCLUDING EGGS, SAUSAGE, BACON, HASHBROWNS, HOT

AND COLD CEREAL, PANCAKES, BAGELS, JUICE AND COFFEE! GIVE YOURSELF A GREAT START WITH A BREAKFAST WORTH WAKING UP FOR! MAGGIE'S COFFEE IS ALWAYS FRESH-BREWED AND THE JUICE FRESH-SQUEEZED. STOP IN TODAY AT MAGGIE'S ON ROUTE 11 IN NORTH SYRACUSE.

:30 Second/Image Message

WHEN YOU'RE NOT QUITE AWAKE, AND NOT QUITE READY TO DRIVE TO WORK, STOP AT MAGGIE'S ON ROUTE 11 IN NORTH SYRACUSE FOR A HOMESTYLE BREAKFAST — COOKED JUST THE WAY YOU LIKE IT. MAGGIE'S ALSO HAS A BREAKFAST BAR FIT FOR A KING INCLUDING EGGS, SAUSAGE, BACON, HASHBROWNS, HOT AND COLD CEREAL, PANCAKES, BAGELS, JUICE AND COFFEE FOR ONLY FIVE NINETY-NINE! GIVE YOURSELF A GREAT START WITH A BREAKFAST WORTH WAKING UP FOR! MAGGIE'S COFFEE IS ALWAYS FRESH-BREWED AND THE JUICE FRESH-SQUEEZED. STOP IN TODAY AT MAGGIE'S ON ROUTE 11 IN NORTH SYRACUSE.

:30 Second/Motivational Message

WHEN YOU'RE NOT QUITE AWAKE, AND NOT QUITE READY TO DRIVE TO WORK, STOP AT MAGGIE'S ON ROUTE 11 IN NORTH SYRACUSE FOR A HOMESTYLE BREAKFAST — COOKED JUST THE WAY YOU LIKE IT. MAGGIE'S ALSO HAS A BREAKFAST BAR FIT FOR A KING INCLUDING EGGS, SAUSAGE, BACON, HASHBROWNS, HOT AND COLD CEREAL, PANCAKES, BAGELS, JUICE AND COFFEE. AND ON WEDNESDAYS, FOR A LIMITED TIME ONLY, YOU'LL GET THAT BREAKFAST BAR FOR ONLY THREE NINETY-NINE! JUST THREE NINETY-NINE! MAGGIE'S COFFEE IS ALWAYS FRESH-BREWED AND THE JUICE FRESH-SQUEEZED. TRY MAGGIE'S ON WEDNESDAYS — ROUTE 11 IN NORTH SYRACUSE.

In truth, all commercials are motivational to some degree. No one designs a message that will turn customers away. Some commercials are just more motivational than others. So even copy we call "strict" image pieces, are meant to interest the consumer. The motivational pieces just blatantly present compelling reasons to see, visit, purchase, or order now rather than later.

5

Television

Television is said to be intrusive with its sight, sound, and motion. It comes right into your home and makes itself the center of attention. How many people settle into a comfy chair with a cup of coffee and stare at their radio with undivided attention?

The newspaper lays on the table until someone picks it up, but the television shouts "Hey! Look at me!"

Television segments a broadcast day in two ways: As specific *types* of programming, such as primetime, daytime, early news, late news, sports, specials, late fringe and children's shows, and by *dayparts*: **Morning** (5:30 AM – 9 AM/Monday - Friday), **Daytime** (9 AM – 4 PM/Monday - Friday), **Early Fringe** (4 PM – 7 PM Monday - Friday), Access (7 PM – 8 PM Saturday and Sunday), **Primetime** (8 PM – 11 PM Monday - Saturday and 7 PM – 11 PM on Sunday), and **Late Fringe** (any regularly scheduled programming after 11:30 PM Monday - Friday) all based on EST.

Television programming uses the following demographics: Women 18+, Women 18–49, Women 55+, Men 18+, Men 18–49, Men 55+. While these ages do not match up perfectly with the choices in the Customer Information Section, they will fit into those categories and your rep can choose the appropriate programs for you from your Group A and Group B choices.

In the 1950s advertisers sponsored entire programs — Kraft Television Theater, the Colgate Comedy Hour, etc. As the cost of production and sponsoring escalated, shared sponsoring occurred, where the announcer would say "This portion of (whatever show) is being brought to you by …."

Even that became too expensive and the popular way to advertise went to :60 second commercials that would run throughout different programs or time slots.

Now the standard for almost all television spots is :30 and sometimes :60 seconds long.

Although there are many television stations to choose from in any given market, television advertising differs from radio in a very basic way. Whereas each radio station has a very distinct audience demographically, one television station can reach every conceivable demographic. Every hour of every day can hold programming for a different audience. Cartoons, sports, news, the soaps, game shows, talk shows, movies, late night, and on and on. By selecting these types of programs you can easily target your desired customer. With the combination of sight and sound in your television commercial, you will come as close as possible to giving your desired customer a personal demonstration of your product or service.

While each local network affiliate rep, or account executive, will be prepared to sell you time on only one station, your cable rep will have many different stations to choose from. And while each network affiliate can target almost any demographic group depending on what programs you choose, each cable station in its entirety will target a certain group. While you might find your local networks are sold out in a particular business quarter, cable can almost always find appropriate space for you on one or more of its many stations. Cable adds frequency to network television schedules at a lower cost and lets you target key demographics with its specialized station programming. You may find that cable is more affordable if you are just getting into television. But check with everyone for the best rates.

Frequency in television advertising is just as critical as it is in radio. The greatest commercial is worthless if no one sees it. Audiences are bombarded with 20–30 commercials for every one hour of programming. If you cannot afford to run a minimum of 10–12 spots per week on any one station, you would be well advised to use another form of advertising. This does not mean 10–12 commercials every week for 52 weeks. But you should run a minimum of 3–4 consecutive weeks when you do advertise.

A specialty business, a golf store for instance, can get around using that many commercials by placing ads into specialty programs, such as televised golf tournaments. The advertiser is guaranteed the right audience and does not have to worry about saturating the market with high frequency, and he has a captive audience. What could be better?!

If you are promoting a sale or a grand opening, use a minimum of 18 spots on each of 2 or 3 stations and just run the ad the week of the event. It's helpful if you can start 3–4 days prior to the event itself and continue through the morning of the event's final day.

You may use *flight* schedules, which means 2–6 weeks of advertising at a time, several times a year — often used by seasonal advertisers, *maintenance* schedules, meaning long-term, low-frequency schedules used for frequently purchased products or services with no seasonal aspect to them, or *pulsing*, which is a schedule of one week on, one week off — or two weeks on and two weeks off. Keeping in mind that two weeks is the average length of time a person remembers an ad, decide which type of schedule will best suit your business.

When you buy the same position (perhaps the 1st slot in the last commercial break of the news) on all three network affiliates, it's called *roadblocking*. This buy gives you, in effect, everyone watching television at that particular time. It's especially effective for news and soap opera programming where there are no reruns and large, loyal audiences. You will pay top dollar for a roadblock, but it is very effective. If you like that idea, but don't want to pay so much, buy any position within the same hour on all three network affiliates. Because most stations carry soaps and news at the same time, it's basically the same thing.

If you can only afford to advertise on one station, ask your television reps for their ratings of the programs you are interested in (news, soaps, cartoons, etc.) and see where the largest audiences are. This rating information will probably come from A.C. Nielsen, the largest national television rating service. Television audience *potential* is based on HUT (households using television) and PUT (persons using television). Television ratings are usually based on *estimated* ratings — or how many households or persons are expected to tune in to a particular program based on how many tuned into previously aired, similar shows.

When completed, your Television Worksheets will list only programs directed to your specific audience. You can choose to use only those programs, or you can include those shows in a *run of schedule* (ROS). An ROS is a schedule created of many or all dayparts, where some of your commercials will run in programs other than those on your list of preferred shows. These schedules can offer increased frequency at the same or comparable rate. Ask your rep to prepare two schedules for your particular budget. One using only your listed target shows and one using an ROS, but including shows on the list. Put the two schedules side-by-side and compare how many of your target programs are in the ROS schedule. You may find that the number is close enough to accept the ROS schedule with more spots at a competitive rate.

A good rule of thumb to use in making this decision is to judge by the total amount of television advertising you do. If you are an infrequent advertiser who buys with small budgets, it's better to hit only programs on your preferred list to be sure each commercial finds a home with the correct audience. If you are a consistent user of television, using ROS as part of your schedule can bring you extra frequency. When inventory is tight, your ROS spots will end up in the least popular shows. But during first and third quarters, you may hit some hot programming for a fraction of the normal cost.

Ask your reps about adding some :10 second spots into your schedule. It adds frequency and keeps the cost down. Don't run :10 second spots alone. They have more impact when used in combination with :30s or :60s.

You should think about increasing reach in your schedules when:

• Your store begins to carry a new, popular brand.
• You open a new location or move your one location.
• Changes in store policies such as in-store financing, delivery or mail order service.
• A large sale or special event.
• Anytime you begin to use a new advertising medium.

Trade: Television stations, like radio stations, have the need for products and services for themselves. There will be fewer requests for trade advertising from television than there will be from radio, however you should let your reps know up front if you are interested in these opportunities when they come along. Gift certificates for restaurants, hotels, tickets to concerts, movies and plays, limousine service, auto repair, business machines, office furniture and cleaning, vehicles for their news department or cars for management and their care, and products for on-air promotions are only a fraction of items and services a station will trade for advertising. Remember to use your highest retail price or hourly rate when figuring out a trade agreement — the station(s) will not be figuring in a cut rate for the cost of their air time. And put an end date on all gift certificates, trade contracts or other paperwork so it is clear when your responsibilities are over.

Production: Your rep can give you suggestions and prices on production choices. For instance, it's less expensive to produce a basic commercial using 8 x 10 photos then it is for the camera crew to come to your location to shoot an hour of footage and then go back to the studio for editing.

However, if you decide to have a camera crew come to you, have them save all of the raw footage. You can use different portions of it later for a new spot without having to pay them to come back. It is not acceptable to use your own personal equipment to shoot the video. There are minimum standards, required by the FCC, that must be met by the stations regarding the quality of the commercials they run and you don't want a slick national spot to run right before your partially-focused ad.

Some of the items that make television production so expensive are the cost of on-location shoots, special effects or animation, elaborate sets, professional casting and celebrity talent fees, extensive editing, and the writing and production of original music.

When working on a tight budget, one of the best spots to produce is one with :20 seconds of generic script and video and :10 seconds of blank tape at the end. That way you can use the same spot over and over by having only the last :10 seconds altered. And if the last :10 seconds of video permanently shows your company's logo, address and phone number, it's faster and less expensive yet to have only the audio (voice) changed.

While :30 seconds has been the standard length for a local television spot, the :60 second spot has begun to emerge as length of choice for the category of automobiles and some large grocery chains, in particular. Over the last two to three years, clients with large budgets have tried to pull themselves above the clutter of their competition by increasing the length of their spots. The next time you're watching television, have a stopwatch available to check the length of various commercials. Also have with you a notepad and pen or pencil. Write down the number and types of commercials you see during a given one hour period. Multiply this by the number of hours you normally watch television in a day and consider the messages you see in that period of time. I think you'll be surprised.

If you are interested in running :60 second television spots, ask your rep(s) what the cost will be. Depending on your geographic location, your :60 may or may not be double the cost of a :30. The cost will vary from station to station in your area as well. Since this book is aimed at the small business owner, I am concentrating on the use of :30 second spots. You would have to have an enormous budget to pay double the cost for the same number of spots in a schedule (remember frequency does not change with the increased length of the spots). If you could afford to run your television schedules with :60 second spots, you could afford an advertising agency!

Your sales rep will assist you in preparing for the production of your commercial. Inquire as to the hourly rate at each station and, if you will be using more than one station, have the spot produced where they charge the least. Your rep will assist you in writing the copy and can make suggestions for music and a voice. If you are running radio along with your television, keep the script the same. You can supply your television production people with a master copy of your radio spot (usually on a reel or CD — not a cassette) to be used as the audio portion of your television commercial.

If you want to be present during the actual production, just ask. It's an interesting process to watch and it will give you the chance for input while the work is in progress. It will take less time than going back to make changes after production in finished. Feel free to suggest changes in the visuals or the written copy. Be satisfied with the final product!

If you are only using one station, you may not have to pay a talent fee. But if you want to run it on another station, you will have to pay a talent fee to the person who voices your spot, as well as for each copy ("dub") of the spot. If your talent is a highly visible personality, such as the station's weatherman or sportscaster, you may not be able to take that commercial to another station at all. It's less hassle and less expensive to use a nonfamous voice.

Unlike radio, where you can fax a script to each station and receive free production, it would be too costly at hundreds (even thousands) of dollars each, to have more than one television station produce a separate version of the same commercial. When making your generic :30, make a :10 while you're there if you think you might want to use one. It's less expensive in the long run to do as much production as possible in one sitting.

Come to production prepared! Since you're being charged by the hour, you'll save money if you have finalized the copy, and decided on the talent and music ahead of time (perhaps you're using your radio commercial as the audio). If you are using photos, you should send them to the station several days in advance along with a clean copy of your logo, your address and phone number, and business hours. If you are shooting at your location, decide ahead of time what you want in the commercial. Do a dress rehearsal if you have to in order to waste as little time as possible at the actual event. Props should be discussed, located, and brought to the studio or your location at least two days ahead to avoid last minute delays that could ruin your schedule.

Keep the master reels at your location in the same place you store your radio spots. Label each box with the name and date of the commercial and keep a typed copy of the script in the box so you can review prices, etc. if you think you want to use it again.

Contracts: The rates for each program listed on your completed Television Worksheets are like the stickers on new cars. Use them as a starting point and always ask for a better price. Don't hesitate to let your reps know you are checking around for a better rate!

Television Worksheet

HAVE YOUR REP FILL OUT AND RETURN THIS SHEET.

Note to Rep: Include only programs geared to the demographics indicated below.

Station ___WWWX___   Dial Position ___Channel 6___

Rep's Name: ___Jane Doe___   Phone Number: ___555-0000 Fax 555-0001___

Owner: Circle choices from Groups A and B that correspond with page 4.

Group A (age)	**Group B (sex)**
18–34	⟨Female⟩
18–49	Male
⟨25–54⟩	Adults (both male and female)
50+	

Weekdays

Time Period	Program	Price per :30	Price per :10
5A - 7A	Morning News	$ 80	$
7A - 9A	Morning Talk	$ 125	$
noon - 12:30	news	$ 295	$
12:30 - 4P	soaps	$ 125	$
5:30P - 7P	news	$ 300	$
11P - 11:30P	news	$ 450	$
		$	$

Weekends

Time Period	Program	Price per :30	Price per :10
6A - 9A	Weekend news	$ 70	$
9A - 10A	Crafts w/ Sally	$ 75	$
1P - 2P	Women and Business	$ 150	$
4P - 5P	Kids Then and Now	$ 65	$
6P - 7P	news	$ 275	$
11P - 11:30P	news	$ 375	$
		$	$

As with radio, first quarter is the best time to negotiate an annual contract. That can also apply to third quarter, with the exception of stations carrying heavy sports programming. When business is down sales managers are hungry for long term contracts to bolster sagging budgets. Your discounts can kick in at the 13 week, 26 week or 52 week level, but may differ depending on your geographical location. If you commit to running a very low number of commercials (3–4 per week) at one of these discount levels, the same discount may or may not also apply to any additional schedules you run during the life of the contract.

Advertisers whose schedules are interrupted by programming changes, cancellation of unpopular new shows, replacement of regular shows with "specials," or the moving of a show to a new day or time-slot, are taken care of in a variety of ways:

• Make-good spots in comparable time slots will be offered.

• The advertiser's spots can follow the show to the new time.

• Schedule is canceled and a credit or rebate is given.

All advertising units are perishable commodities. Once an empty space has gone by, it cannot be recaptured for sale at another time. While some stations or publications will come down in price at the last minute to sell vulnerable inventory, others will let it go unsold to protect the integrity of the normal rates and also to avoid "backlash buying" from advertisers who then won't go back to paying a higher rate. Actually, none of them try to hit a 100 percent sold out position. They may need the space for make-good spots, trade, last minute schedules, or other situations requiring the use of that extra inventory.

There are always one or two advertisers in any market who negotiate "remnant rates" with an agreeable radio or television station, and newspaper. This must be a client whose product or service has wide appeal and can find an audience at any time, on any day. The contract states that the reps will contact the advertiser at the last minute on a daily or weekly basis and be advised of unsold space. The advertiser agrees to purchase a portion of the unsold space for a specified dollar amount. The contract can indicate a maximum number of commercials per week or per month that the advertiser agrees to buy without notification. Even with the ability to sell time to remnant advertisers, the stations and publications may hold back inventory required to take care of emergencies.

Circle your pre-determined choices from Groups A and B onto the Television Worksheet. Have your account executives complete and return them to you. Unlike your Radio Worksheets, you will keep *all* of your Television Worksheets, because every station will have opportunities for you to reach your target audience. Your salespeople are instructed to list ONLY shows that

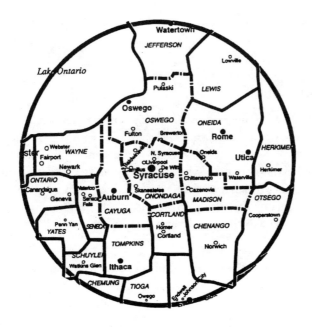

match your specific demographics. Use a separate worksheet for each cable station you are interested in, just as you would for each of the network stations. Once these worksheets are completed, you will have a list of programs watched by your potential customers on both local network and cable stations and you will know at a glance what a :30 second spot in each show costs.

By looking at a coverage map like this one, you can determine if a given television station will be beneficial for your location(s). The large circle shows the outer reaches of the station's signal or TSA (Total Survey Area). Instead of using a smaller circle inside the large one to indicate the lesser, more local area of the MSA (Metro Survey Area), this station has chosen to demonstrate the boundaries of that coverage area with a broken-line symbol.

Please Leave Your Relatives at Home

So, your kids are cute, your brother-in-law is an aspiring actor and wants a shot at being discovered, your sister thinks she can sing, and your dog is almost a person. Leave them at home. It's hard to find a less professional-looking and sounding commercial than one in which a client's family, beloved pet, or even the client himself (or herself) appears. It happens all the time, and it's even a great sales tool. Account Execs from radio and television know that a client will run an ad more often if a member of his or her family is in the commercial. It's an ego thing. Don't do it.

With few exceptions, business owners and their families should stay away from the camera. We don't all look kindly, humorous, cuddly, or even nice — and we're not good judges of how we appear or sound to others. Clearly, we don't want to do anything to impede the production of a crisp, concise, product or service-enhancing ad.

A professional person's appearance and voice will not distract in any way from the intent or message of the commercial. If you have a wiggling child, reciting memorized lines in a monotone, staring at the camera like a deer caught in headlights, you have no chance of having your message received. Similarly, your dog wearing a fisherman's hat or sitting in a recliner with a cigar sticking out of his mouth, eyes darting from side to side like he needs to go out, will totally thwart your commercial message. Even if you have to sneak out of the house, leave them all at home!

Give the script to your radio or television account executive. He or she will recommend an experienced voice and/or personality to provide you with a commercial that will shine the spotlight on your business, product, service, sale, or special event. And if you decide to change the voice for the next spot, the professional won't sulk for days at your dinner table!

Consent and Release

Whenever you produce a television commercial or a promotional video, or develop any kind of print using the image, name, or voice of any person, whether you pay them or not, get a consent and release form signed by each and every one of them. Even if it's your best friend, your business partner, or a member of your own family, it's the smart thing to do. Unfortunately, business partners, friends, and families sometimes split up or have major disagreements. If that happens and your print ad, direct mail piece, outdoor billboard, or commercial happens to include the name, the image or the voice of the angry person, you can be forced to stop using that spot, ad, or design, and incur the expense of producing a new one.

If you are filming in a restaurant, a bar, a store, or in the street, plant the people who will be in the ad and have them sign the form well ahead of the shoot. The area should be secured so that no one else wanders into the camera range. If they do, you must obtain their signature on a consent and release form immediately. The same goes for anyone who poses for print or voices a radio spot.

When choosing talent for any of your advertising, keep in mind that using a famous local personality has disadvantages as well as advantages. Several years ago I produced some Public Service Announcements for a local not-for-profit

Consent and Release Form

With my signature below, I consent to the use of my name, voice, or image for the following:

Business Name: _ABC Restaurant_

Title of spot or ad: _Patio Clambake Fridays_

Dates ad will run: _6/1/98_ to _8/31/98_

☒ Check this box for unlimited use.

☒ I have read and understand this form.

☒ I am 18 years old.

☐ I am the minor child's parent and signing for my child.

☒ I am /am not receiving payment.

☒ I understand this material will not be used for any other purpose.

John Doe	_May 2, 1998_
Signature	Date
12345 Sixth St.	_555-0008_
Address	Phone number
Jane Doe-Smith	_May 2, 1998_
Witness signature	Date

Use one form for each person.

agency. The agency was celebrating a 100 year anniversary in their community and I thought it would be great to have local politicians and broadcast personalities, do :10 second spots wishing the agency well. Before the campaign even began, I had to re-shoot several of the :10s because a couple of the broadcast personalities (2 from radio and 1 from television) changed stations, and one person resigned his political office. This type of production is best for a campaign intended for a single use — one not intended to be used again in the future.

Keep all of your signed consent forms in a file. It's not unusual for a generic spot or ad to be used for months or even years unless a specific end date is written into the agreement, so don't throw the signed consent forms away! Keep them as long as you use the material.

This applies to children, adults, strangers, and people you know. The owners of any animals you use must also sign for the beast(s).

6

Print

Dailies, weeklies, monthlies, quarterlies, tabloid inserts — the list goes on and on. Print is everywhere. You're looking at it right now!

Newspaper and specialty publication advertising have been around longer than any of us, and despite the enormous growth of radio and television advertising, print remains the leading advertising medium. Business people love print ads because they can clip them, hang them on the wall, and 15 years later still read them, touch them, and show them to their grandchildren — while those darn radio and television ads disappear into thin air leaving only the hope that someone was watching or listening when they ran. And it's tough to pay an invoice for something that disappeared into thin air.

That was the thought process of a lot of older business people and many passed the mind set down to the next generation, and so on. Today we see the power of all forms of advertising when they are used properly and we know that print is still a wonderful form of getting out our messages.

Daily newspapers offer constant market presence and are considered time-sensitive because they are generally read on the day of publication. There is a sense of immediacy about this form of advertising because every new day brings new information — and with it — new advertising. Although many people today get their news from television or radio simply because they don't have the time to invest in reading an entire paper, it is one of the best places to reach the older segment of the population which does have the time and the inclination to comb through each page.

The weekly subscription papers in your area are wonderful for covering specific geographic locations — one at a time or all areas at once. People are likely to read a publication they have paid to have delivered or mailed to their home or office, giving these papers an edge over the free shopper publications. The papers are mailed or delivered by newsboys and newsgirls to key suburban areas — and you can choose to advertise in one or all of the available papers. Your rep will provide you with a list of circulation areas and the number of deliverable addresses within each zip code. Each specific paper will carry neighborhood news and information. You can place the same ad in all papers or alter your ad with different products or offers for different zip communities. The more papers you use at one time, the lower your cost will be per ad.

Newspapers provide readers with more specific information on sales, promotions, and events, than can radio or television's vanishing :30 or :60 seconds. Print ads make it easy for consumers to do comparative shopping and to take time reading and re-reading the ads that attract them. This makes newspaper advertising a wonderful partner to radio and television, allowing the rest of the story to be told in greater detail.

Measurement of newspapers is done by circulation. While the circulation figures will tell you how many papers are delivered, the information in somewhat limited in value. The circulation of a paper does not accurately portray the number of actual readers per paper. You are not able to get a handle on how many people read each section or how many people may read one paper delivered to a household or an office. No specific demographics are available. Think of the coverage as potential readership rather than actual readership. And remember that people will usually hang onto a paper long enough to receive the next copy. So dailies are discarded on a daily basis — along with your ad — while weeklies tend to stay around for the whole week.

When using a daily publication, be sure to request the sections of the publication you prefer such as sports, metro, restaurant guide, local news, etc.. If you don't want your ad to show up on the obituary page, be sure and say or it might very well end up there.

For a slight increase in cost, some weeklies will sell one half of their front page and all of their back page to advertisers. If you like that idea, reserve it in advance and ask the cost of adding one color to parts of the ad to draw the reader's eye to it.

Different forms of print cater to a wide variety of consumers. Shopper guides and coupons (whether clipped out of a print ad or received in a direct mail program) do very well for small ticket items and can be counted on to reach people who are looking for a bargain. "Shoppers" are less expensive than your daily or local weekly subscription paper, which is good news for the new business owner on a limited budget.

There are many ways to use print in conjunction with other media. Combining print with radio or television is a great way to not only reach more people, but to reinforce each other's messages. Use radio or television to alert people to direct mail or newspaper ads containing "more information" or coupons redeemable at your place of business. For example, "See Thursday's paper" or "Watch your mailbox this week for money-saving coupons." Ask your rep for creative ways to make your ad stand out on the page.

Magazine advertising is not always the first type of print you think of, but it can give you the ability to reach specialty markets very effectively. There are local magazines you can pick up for free on display in your area in high traffic locations such as grocery and drug stores, mini-marts and gas stations. They range in subjects from real estate, restaurant guides, antique cars, entertainment features such as musical events, movies, and local theater productions, etc., and if their specialty readers are of interest to you, these magazines are a great place to reach them. Pick up one or two copies of any that you can use. The numbers to call for advertising information will be printed in the publication. You can also check with your local Chamber of Commerce for a list of such local magazines.

Many nationally distributed magazines will have local sections you can buy. You may have been looking through a *Time* or *Newsweek* and stopped suddenly at a full page ad for a business in your town. These magazines publish special sections sold on a regional basis. These ads can lend a great deal of credibility to

your business and are a great place for specialty stores because people will travel for great distances to check out a "new" supplier for their hobby. They also serve businesses with more than one location well since their coverage areas are usually broken down into large segments of the country (Northeast, Northwest, Southeast, etc.). Magazines specializing in fishing, specific sports, pets, cars, home decorating, parenting, health, and business are just a few types of nationally distributed magazines that sell local sections. All of them print the phone and fax numbers you will need to call for information in the magazine.

You may be asked to pay cash-in-advance for your ads when you begin to advertise with all media until you establish a credit history, but this is especially true for the print media. When a business becomes strapped for cash, media usually feels the pinch first by being paid late or not at all. Some papers will offer a discount for cash-in-advance, or payment within 15 days. Once you have established a good track record, you will certainly be extended 30-day credit. If, however, you fall behind at some point, you may find yourself back to a cash-in-advance status.

Contracts: Contracts in daily and weekly papers are commonplace because the rate for placing one ad at a time is quite a bit higher than even agreeing to place 2 or 3 ads during one year. Ad sizes are figured in column inches. If you look in any paper, you'll see that the pages are laid out with a certain number of equal-sized columns, each column running straight from the top of the page to the bottom, unless broken by an advertisement. When figuring the size of an ad, you make two "size" determinations:

- How many columns wide to make your ad — you can cover one column, two columns, or all of the columns on a page.
- How many inches long do you want your ad?

Let's say you want your ad to be three columns wide and five inches long. To determine the cost of that ad you multiply three (number of columns wide) by five (the number of inches long). Your ad will be 15 column inches in size. If your chosen publication charges $6.00 per column inch, your ad will cost $90.00 (15 column inches x $6.00). There are price breaks for different numbers of column inches just as there are price breaks for running 24 radio spots instead of 12 in one week. The more print ads you run, the lower the cost per ad will be. Different sections of the paper and special sections may have different rates per column inch.

Your newspaper contract will specify a total number of column inches to be used over a 52 week period — or whatever period of time your contract is for. You may only commit to running a few ads a year and you need not know exactly when you will use them when you sign your contract. As the year progresses, your rep will let you know how many column inches you still must run to fulfill your contract. Some papers offer both frequency discounts (the more often you run) and bulk column inch (the number of ads you run) discounts. If you run more column inches than your contract calls for and actually reach the next price break, you may receive a rebate at the end of the year. If you don't reach your contract level, however, you may be short-rated — meaning you will be billed for the difference between the contract rate (which you did not meet) and the normal rate for the number of column inches you did run.

You need not always run display ads. Retail classified ads are available at a much less expensive rate and appear in the classified section under specific headings. They are short, all-text ads, with no graphics or borders. An example would be:

> **Baby Furniture** — cribs, dressers, changing tables, rocking chairs, lamps, cradles, all 50% off. Sheets, blankets, baby books, diaper bags, and other accessories 25% off now through Sunday at Baby Town, 123 Fourth St.

Layout and Production: Your rep will take the information you provide and create a layout (design) for your approval. Ask to see a proof of your ad before it runs. Check your address, phone number, dates, everything to be sure it's correct. To help your rep have time to plan your design and provide you with a proof in time to make changes, give him or her as much notice as you can — preferably a week or two before deadline.

If your rep is not able to provide you with a proof — and your ad should run incorrectly — if it runs on the wrong day, if the phone number is wrong — call immediately and ask for a make-good ad in the next available paper. If the next available paper is too late for your sale or special event, request a full refund or credit. One of the best reasons to see a proof before publication is to go over the ad with a fine-tooth comb to be sure there are no mistakes in the print.

When writing or approving copy for your print ads, remember that keeping the main idea as simple as possible is the best idea. Determine what message you need to get across and then find the shortest, clearest way to deliver it. Use phrases from daily life that everyone is familiar with to conjure up instant understanding for the reader.

> It's the KISS theory — Keep It Simple Stupid!
> "Please send assistance as soon as humanly possible" or "HELP!"

> "The rabbit died" — "The jig is up" — "You're being sued." — "Stop" — "Yes, I'm lost" — "The money's gone"— "Bobby threw up" — "This is a stick-up"

These short phrases are easy to understand. Keep your main message simple, and understandable — then use it over and over in print as well as all of your other media ads.

Think about the commercials on radio and television, in print or on billboards that you have remembered, have made you laugh, or actually motivated you to take action and go to the store or business advertised. Over the years, clients have told me they thought it was great when other businesses were really creative, but that they didn't feel it was something they wanted to do in their own advertising. That sentiment is the reason why some of the best ideas can be found in agency trash cans. If you are lucky enough to have a rep with a fertile imagination (whether it's your print, radio, or television rep), ask for help in coming up with something unusual, entertaining, funny, or a little off-the-wall, and then turn him or her loose. Remember, you are not bound to use whatever may result — but you might find that you want to. Your reps can show you samples of great ads to get you thinking.

The completed Print Worksheet will tell you everything you need to know about any publication you use. Since you may not want to do the column-inch-math each time you go to buy print, it's good to have this worksheet for reference purposes. Keep all of the sheets completed by your print salespeople for fast, easy reference.

Have Fun With Your Ads!

**Use Color!
It attracts the reader's eye!**

Use color for attention!

**Use Reverse Print
(white letters on black)
It shows up!**

Use reverse print — white letters on a black background for sharp contrast.

Use Different Fonts
They make your ad unique!

Unusual fonts will bring your print ads to life and add interest.

Tip: If your print ads, coupons, and direct mail pieces are aimed at the older population (50+), use a slightly larger print than you normally would.

Tip: Save postage by inserting information on upcoming sales, new products or services, or special events to existing customers in their monthly invoice envelopes.

Tip: You cannot create a "lottery" situation in a contest with any media. If your contest contains three things: Chance, a prize, and consideration (money), you have the makings of a lottery and will not be allowed to advertise it. The three magic words to keeping your contest legal are: NO PURCHASE REQUIRED. Government lotteries are exempt.

Print Worksheet

HAVE YOUR REP FILL OUT AND RETURN THIS SHEET.

Publication ___Daily Paper___ Phone Number ___555-7771___

Rep's Name: ___John Doe___

☒ Daily   ☐ Weekly   ☐ Other

Ad Size	Price	Day Ad Would Run
Full Page	$ 4,000	6/9/98
1/2 Page	$ 2,000	
1/4 Page	$ 1,000	
1/8 Page	$ 500	
Other	$	

Deadline for copy ___6/1/98___

Cost of adding one color ___$150___   2 colors: ___#215___

Special Sections Geared to this Business

Summer	Fall	Winter	Spring
Home and Gardern	Energy Efficient	Holiday	Flowers and
	Homes	Decorating	Shrubs
Vacation Special			

Contract rate per column inch: $ ___14.50___

Contract start date: ___Jan. 1, 1997___   End date: ___Jan. 31, 1993___

7

Direct Mail

When you come home at the end of the work day, one of the first things you do — and everyone does — is go through your mail. While you may or may not keep everything in the pile, you definitely look at each piece of mail to determine what it is. On a daily basis, your bills, letters, bank statements, and magazines will almost always be accompanied by one or more pieces of direct mail in the form of individual coupons, surveys, flyers, or in envelopes, stuffed with offers from many different businesses. Perhaps the irony of receiving all of these pieces of mail together has escaped you. That is — those direct mail pieces that found their way to your mailbox, originated from businesses who purchased your name and address from one or all of the other companies represented in that pile of mail.

Direct Mail Works Well for Different Types of Businesses

First, let's look at the coupons and offers you receive in envelopes every month from national mailers like Val-Pak and Carol Wright. These coupon packs, referred to as cooperative direct mail, are sent to specific zip codes through local and national direct mail companies (check the Yellow Pages under Advertising — direct). These envelopes are stuffed full of colorful coupon offers from 20 or 30 different businesses and go out to certain zip codes on a specific monthly schedule. They offer budget-friendly production packages in one-color to four-color printing on glossy or non-glossy paper. The paper is offered in white or color, and you can have one or both sides of your coupon printed. Your price should include design, layout, proof, typesetting, insertion, labels, envelopes, and postage. Your total cost will depend on the production choices you make and how many areas you wish to cover with the mailing.

While this grouping of coupons may not be your absolute first choice, mailing this way does have one advantage: it allows you to send out greater numbers of coupons and cover more area for less money than you can by doing your own individual mailing. The practical price you pay is that the recipients who actually keep and open the envelopes will have to sort through all of the other material to find your piece. You also must be aware that many zip codes are made up of clusters of high, middle, and low income dwellers. Depending on your offering, large percentages of the mailing may not end up in the hands of your targeted consumer.

To use this form of direct mail, you must get hold of the current schedule of each company to see which month(s) will cover the zip codes you want. Your reps from these companies will be happy to fax, mail, or drop by with their schedules.

If these envelopes in your area have a "full-view window" on the front, you can buy the window placement — in other words, a portion of your coupon would show through the window for the recipients to see before the envelope was opened. If you have your coupon designed so that the section showing through the window is very clever, or teases the person into opening the envelope, you're going to get a higher rate of return on your investment because more people will at least read your mailing. The company reps will help you design your coupons for the window and show you samples to spark your imagination. It will cost a little more to buy the window position, but it is definitely worth it if you handle it right! Above all, it's the offer itself that becomes so important in this type of direct mail attempt.

This cooperative form of direct mail:

- Can give you higher volume of pieces mailed at an affordable price.
- A great design (in the window) can make it more closely resemble an individual mailing.

Historically, these types of coupon mailings work better for lower-priced items such as dry cleaners, pizza and wings, car washes, lawn and garden shops, restaurants, rug or home cleaning, driveway installation and repair, etc. Free appraisal coupons work well for real estate and remodeling companies, hardwood floor installation and the like.

Another option is to use a direct mail company (also called a mail house) that will design, print, and mail your own individual piece to your desired zip codes. They can separate residence from business addresses or just blanket one or more areas so that every address within your chosen zip codes receives your mailing.

Direct mail of this sort is available in postcard-size to larger, very fancy pieces with several pages or panels and you can mail them whenever you like without having to wait for a pre-determined schedule. Although it costs more to mail this way — because many of the costs are fixed — such as postage, paper, and the cost of printing, the advantages may be worth it to you. Not only do you have control over the timing of the mailing, but your message or offer will not be put into an envelope with other businesses for the recipient to dig through to find your direct mail piece — you have exclusivity.

This type of mailing works well for all businesses with one or more locations, high-end retail, specialty stores and ones with business-to-business material. Catalogs, brochures, and postage-paid response cards can all be specifically targeted for you with direct mail. When you send out postage-paid response cards, you only pay return postage on the pieces you get back. You can use this method of advertising as an introduction for a new business or service, or to open doors for sales calls.

You may find that dollar-for-dollar, you enjoy better results with targeted direct mail — especially if you can combine it with radio or television. When you do, get your mailing out slightly ahead of your electronic advertising or right at the same time. Your commercial message should alert listeners to check their mail for the coupons or offers. Let them know when they can expect to receive them and what the benefit of those coupons will be.

If you like the idea of individual direct mail pieces, but the cost of postage makes sending out large quantities prohibitive, have your flyers or coupons printed by the direct mail companies and use them as inserts in daily or weekly papers.

Most daily papers have a "neighborhood" or local section delivered with the main paper or mailed separately. While the main body of a daily paper carries the same information to its entire circulation, the neighborhood sections print very specific news of individual towns, and are only circulated to addresses within those towns. You can control the number of flyers you print and distribute by choosing the specific areas you want to target and having your flyers or coupons inserted into those specific neighborhood sections.

If your daily paper has a minimum number of insertions too large for your budget (you will be charged a fee-per-thousand-pieces) try your weekly papers. You will most likely have a choice between a subscription paper — one that people actually pay to have delivered to their homes — and a "shopper" publication delivered to homes for free. Both will let you insert flyers or coupons into specific areas for a certain price-per-thousand. Either one will be less expensive than the daily paper.

Think about what your offer is saying, the prices you are quoting, the people you want to reach, and make your choice. If your weekly paper or shopper cannot print the inserts for you, have a direct mail company or your own printer do them. Get your delivery deadline and have them there on time!

When your daily paper is unaffordable, you should know that:

• Many experts think that the subscription weekly gives you the best shot at having your insert seen because people read publications they pay for. And you can feel comfortable using these subscription weeklies for higher priced items. These subscriptions generally go to higher income households. You can sell the offer and the benefit of your product or service to these consumers.

• The "shopper" paper is better for readers who are looking for a bargain. A combination of an ad — or insert — in the free weekly "shopper" publication and coupons in an envelope-style mailing will work well together to target the same bargain hunters for a comparatively low cost. Sell a great offer to these buyers — forget the benefit. No high ticket items or services should be advertised in "shoppers."

Direct mail companies work from lists compiled from several sources to break down their targets not only by zip code, but also by separating residence from business addresses. They can provide psychographic and demographic information such as income, number of children, and education levels mentioned in other sections of this book. As I stated before, I have reservations about the value of psychographic information. However, your direct mail company has vast resources when it comes to obtaining lists compiled according to the habits of individuals, such as magazine subscriptions, club memberships, store purchases, and even by credit reporting services who will sell lists of people according to how many credit cards they have, and by how quickly (or slowly) they pay their bills! This information is reliable, because it has been gathered according to what people do without thinking — according to how they live their lives. When getting ready to do a local mailing, use your knowledge of your community, and mail to those zip codes you feel will supply the best response to your product and offer.

Call the Chamber of Commerce offices in areas you would like to penetrate and ask what the cost of inserting flyers into their monthly mailings would be. They will often have a program to insert hundreds of flyers into monthly mailings to members for as little as $50 — great for business-to-business as well as business-to-consumer advertising. Admittedly, not everyone who receives a monthly mailing from the Chamber of Commerce, or from any other source, actually reads the whole piece each month. Sometimes secretaries or office managers pull out only what they think will be of interest to their bosses — and sometimes the mailings get buried on a messy desk. Get a list of the Chamber members, select the names or businesses you feel are outstanding prospects for your product or service and make some phone calls a day or two ahead of the scheduled delivery to tell those prime prospects that the flyer is on its way. Then, if they're interested, they will be sure to look for it.

While this type of insertion fee may be low, you will have to pay a printer to produce your material. Your printer will be able to help you with the design and layout of your piece. Don't do it yourself — especially when you're just starting out. You want the material to look professional. Remember that everything you put into the community says something about you and your company. Trying to save on production will not be a savings in the long run if your stuff looks unprofessional.

Direct Mail and "Mail Back" Offers

Reply sections of your mailings or inserts can be easily designed for people who are interested in making an appointment, receiving a free estimate, taking advantage of a discount, or entering a contest by filling in their name and address and mailing the card back to you.

Whatever kind of direct mail you use, put a lot of thought into its design and content. Consider the fact that you have only 2–4 seconds to get the reader's attention. Think about what kind of coupons you like to receive. Do you look at those printed on colorful paper with black lettering? What coupon offers are you more likely to hang on to and use? Turn your thoughts to your customer and decide what kind of an offer will provide enough motivation to keep him or her reading. Once you decide, repeat the offer 3–4 times.

Immediacy is important! The shorter the offer period is, the faster you will realize a response. Remember to put an end date on all of your mailings. If you don't give your offers a definite limit, you will find yourself honoring them for the rest of your life.

There are many possible dramatic and clever combinations with color, fonts, and graphics you can use to create a direct mail piece that will catch someone's eye or peak their curiosity about the rest of the message. Don't let yours be the one that gets passed by or thrown out with nothing more than a glance because it looks flat or has too many words on it. Listen to the advice of your rep who does this for a living. Use the experience he or she brings to your project.

And, as with everything else, make sure your logo is on every piece of direct mail you send out, along with your address, phone and fax numbers, and business hours if they are out of the ordinary. Request a "proof" of your ad before it hits the mail and check it carefully to be sure all of the information is correct. Don't leave anything to chance. Check, check, and check again.

Coupons and other types of direct response mail are some of the best types of advertising for tracking results. It is a very common practice for business owners to ask customers where they heard about his or her company. The customer, who has come into your store for a particular reason, (#1) does not want to be side-tracked by that sort of a question — and quite honestly, you should not want to sidetrack that customer from looking for something to purchase — and (#2) does not realize how important the answer is. He will say the first thing that comes to mind ("the Yellow Pages" or "the newspaper" are the two most common answers) so he can get on with the business at hand.

With coupons or mail-backs, you will know exactly where the coupons came from. If you are using more than one publication for your inserts, have an identifying mark or change the wording or the offer slightly so you know immediately where the coupon was found.

When filled out by your rep(s), the Direct Mail Worksheet will provide the details you need to know to make an informed decision before you agree to this type of campaign.

Direct Mail Worksheet

Company Name ABC Direct Mail   Sales Rep: __David Doe__

Address: ___1234 7th St.___   Phone Number: __555-8881__

___Omaha, Nebraska___   Fax: __555-8882__

☐ Mailings   ☒ Inserts

If inserts, name of publication: __Daily Paper__   Publication date: __6/8/98__

Insertion cost per thousand: __$50__

Postage cost if mailing: _____   Mailing date: _____

Zip codes/areas covered: __all__

Number of pieces: __50,000__   Size of pieces: __8½" x 10"__

How many colors/what specific colors: __(2) black and yellow__

Deadline for final design and copy: __5/29/98__

Date of proof: __6/1/98__   Changes made: __corrected phone number__

__added expiration date__

_____

_____

Final approval date: __6/2/98__

Total cost (including postage or insertion charge, tax, etc.) $ __2,500__

Details of this direct mail campaign: __coupon offering__

Offer or sale: __Buy one meal, get one free__

End date on offer: __6/30/98__

8

Outdoor Advertising

If you have a sign over your business door, you already believe in outdoor advertising and have started using it. Now you have to decide how many people should see your sign — or one like it. Are the people who drive by your door every day enough or do you also need to reach people who don't normally use the road in front of your business? Obviously, you need to reach many more people than those who pass by on their way home each day.

One way to accomplish that is to take advantage of billboards placed along well-traveled routes 10–20 miles or even up to 40–50 miles away from your location. Lighted billboards promote your business and location up to 18 hours a day and are seen time and time again by the people who constantly drive by them. Billboards can be purchased by the month or on long term contracts. They are available in several different sizes — along two-lane roads as well as superhighways. You can buy one or two billboards and have them moved from one location to another on a rotary program or your can buy groups of boards called a *showing* and have them all up at one time in various locations. A showing can offer 25, 50, 75, or even 100 percent of daily coverage of the daily driving public. The number of boards you need to achieve these percentages depends on your location, the number of roads leading to your location, and the number of boards you can afford. Most outdoor companies have a variety of programs to accommodate different budgets.

Outdoor advertising experts sight several reasons why this form of advertising is growing:

• The expanded use of VCRs and the fragmentation of television audiences due to the increase in the number of available stations — both network and cable — make television advertising more of a long shot than it used to be.

- The high cost of trying to cover a specific demographic adequately on available radio stations.
- The dramatic cost increase many local markets experience in newspaper advertising while readership in many of those same markets is declining.
- The increased mobility of today's population — making highways and neighborhood roads perfect places for your message.

Outdoor advertising can be the final reminder to your customer of your product or service. It bridges the gap between the advertising message heard in the home and the actual purchase at your business location. And because of its continuous presence (you can't turn it off or hit a fast-forward button to get rid of it) outdoor advertising produces frequency levels unmatched by other media. Billboards truly keep your message alive long after the paper has been thrown out and the radio and television have been turned off. Billboards serve as a constant reminder to the established local traffic, and an immediate first notice to one-time tourists or people who have recently moved into the area.

It's one place that your business can appear to be as big as the largest national company. Billboards come in three basic sizes and everyone who uses outdoor appears on one of them. It's the great equalizer. Outdoor billboards can also enhance other forms of advertising you may do:

- Combine outdoor advertising with newspaper to not only keep your one-time print ad going all day long, but to increase its size and add color to it as well.
- Combine outdoor advertising with your radio schedules to add visual presence with bold graphics and the 8–10 most powerful and recognizable words of your radio copy. (Radio plus outdoor used to be knows as "poor man's television.")
- Combine outdoor advertising with your television campaign to reach fragmented audiences and put back the impact lost by channel zappers.

Billboards work well for specialty shops and high-ticket outdoor items like motorcycles, snowmobiles, riding lawnmowers, and automobiles, as well as tires, oil change and tune-up locations, car washes, and anything to do with a car. After all, the customer is sitting in the vehicle that needs those new tires, is making a funny noise, or could use a good washing as he or she passes your message on the road. Perfect for that impromptu purchase.

Don't overlook the directional advantages of outdoor billboards. They are perfect for directing traffic right to your door if you can find one or more nicely located boards on which you can place your logo with an arrow and a directional message. This type of board is very helpful if you can leave it up all year long. Ask your outdoor rep for long term contract discount information.

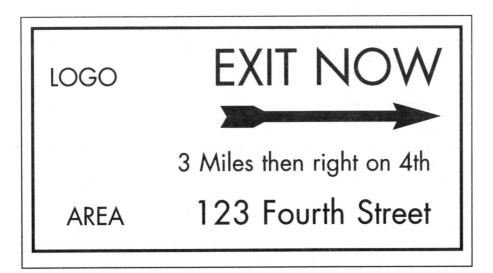

Your billboards can be placed in strategic locations reaching everyone coming into or going out of your market area. Your rep will show you a map of streets and highways in your area with board locations. From this map you can determine which boards will best serve your advertising needs. If you can't afford to put a board on every street leading to your business door, buy one or two billboards on a rotary program and have them periodically moved to the other appropriate sites.

Photo courtesy of Coleman's Authentic Irish Pub, Syracuse, NY.

Outdoor's large physical characteristics — big, bold and colorful — create a great visual impact on your audience. For this reason, your creative efforts should be consideration #1 when deciding what your boards will look like.

Many outdoor companies employ a creative director who will help you with content and design. If not, your rep will aid you in choosing a layout and deciding on the copy for your board(s).

The Outdoor Worksheet has a space for your rep to show you what your board will look like before you finalize a design and get into production. He or she should be able to provide you with samples of award-winning boards from around the world to get your imagination going!

There are several methods of producing your designs in paper, paint and vinyl. One will surely fit your budget. As with other forms of advertising, if you are working with a limited budget, don't choose the most expensive form of production. Put the lion's share of the budget into the number of boards, and use a less expensive form of production.

Production

Your worksheet will indicate production charges for your board(s) — that is, how much the paint, paper, or vinyl (flex) used on them will cost. The production fee is billed over and above the monthly rental charge. If your boards will be up long-term, you should know that paint stays beautiful for up to one year, the vinyl flex lasts for 2–3 years — both longer than paper, which usually needs changing every 45–60 days. The cost of poster (paper) production is determined by the number of colors you use and the numbers of posters you print. When using paper, have a few extra posters printed at the beginning in case vandalism or weather damage occurs. It's less expensive to print a few extra with the first printing than to have 1 or 2 more done at a later date.

Paint and Vinyl Production

Vinyl flex is the newest form of production. Designs are computer generated or painted onto a large sheet of vinyl which is then slipped over the board like a large pillowcase and tightened in the back. Photo reproductions work well on vinyl flex — the finished product is more life-like and three-dimensional than with painted boards or with paper. Using computer generated photos in your design is expensive. However, depending on the number of units you purchase, you may be able to negotiate free paint production on the vinyl. With paint you can have graphics in your design, but not photo reproduction.

Extras

Cut-outs on painted boards give your overall design movement, extra dimension, and a larger, more exciting appearance. For a minimal $-per-square-foot charge (cost will vary depending on your geographical area), you can take your design off the four straight sides of your board(s) in any or all of the four directions. The top one-third of a wine bottle can tower above the board. An elephant's trunk or the front end of a car can reach over one side of the board to create the illusion of movement. Again, your rep can show you samples of boards with cut-outs as part of their design. See the example below of a cut-out in the board designed for Thunder Island.

Solar rays — small foil-like discs that shake in the wind — attach at their centers to critical areas of your board to create a sparkle effect. Available in silver, gold, and many other colors, these light-throwers work very well in areas where a lot of sun shines.

Poster Production

Your design can be generated from a photo negative, or done with *flat tones* — which means you can still have illustrations, but they have a less realistic appearance (and are less expensive to use) than a photograph. Your rep can show you

Photo courtesy of Thunder Island, Fulton, NY.

samples of each. If you have co-op available to you from a supplier, ask if pre-printed posters exist. A phone call can put them in your hands overnight and wipe out most of the production costs you would otherwise pay. They will arrive fully printed with the exception of a blank section at the bottom for your logo and address, which will be imprinted by your outdoor company.

One way to keep your 30-sheet poster billboard(s) current, is to make use of *imprints* — or large stickers — across a specific section of the board. If you start

Example of "teaser boards."

Photos courtesy of WIXT-TV, Syracuse, NY

with a generic board for a flower shop full of colorful blooms and copy that says "THINK FLOWERS ALL YEAR LONG" you can cover the ALL YEAR LONG section with an imprint (like a big bumper-sticker) that reads "Valentine's Day — Feb. 14th," then "Easter," then cover that one up with one that says "Mother's Day" and the date in May. You can usually go four layers deep before you have to worry about new production.

Teaser boards are very popular — but they can be expensive unless you do them cleverly. Usually, teaser boards require two full sets of posters to be printed. The first design gives a provocative message with no sponsoring logo.

The second gives the rest of the message and the logo. You can use the first set of posters, or teaser portion, for the first 10 days of a 30 day contract and then put the second set with the remainder of the message up for the last 20 days. Because posters are made up of printed top and bottom sections, ask your rep to print just one set and post the top half of the board (teaser section) for the first 10 days and the post the bottom half day 11 through the end of the month with the punch line. For instance:

(Days 1 - 10)

YOUR HUSBAND KNOWS

(Day 11) -

IT'S TIME FOR WINTER TIRES!

LOGO SECTION

ADDRESS AND PHONE NUMBER

Keep your boards simple and bright. Remember that people go by them quickly so the artwork should be colorful and the message short — no more than 8–10 words plus your logo section. I know that when you're paying for advertising space you want to put as much information as you can in an ad, but that is not the way billboards work. There's only so much information people in a moving vehicle can absorb. I have worked with people who would have been happy to put the Lord's Prayer and their mother's maiden name on their posters, and it's hard to get some clients to stick to the 8–10 word rule. But if you do, and you make those 8–10 words powerful, you'll be fine. It will provide you with "top of the mind awareness" with the consumer so that when your product or service is needed, your business name will be the one that springs to mind.

Drive by the available boards and see if they are easily seen from the road. Are they clearly visible or obstructed by trees? Often, a board that cannot be seen in the summer because of the trees can be clearly seen in the winter after the leaves have fallen. Take note of the colors on the boards that catch your eye. Often there will be a series of 3 or more boards attached to each other in a grouping. Which of the three boards did you notice first? Perhaps the one closest to the road? Or the center board because its color and design made it stand out from the others?

When determining whether to buy east or west facing boards (or north or south facing), choose billboards that people will see while driving *towards* your location(s) — not when they're driving away from you for "impulse products." The time to attract their attention is when they still have the opportunity to look for your store or office and it's convenient to stop because they happened to be in the neighborhood. If there are no boards in the "correct" position, or if you're waiting for one to become available, use a board in close proximity but facing the opposite way until something better comes along. You don't want to give up the traffic in that area altogether while you're waiting. Boards for higher ticket items like cars, vacations, furniture, etc. can face any direction.

If you are renting lighted boards, drive by them occasionally at night to be sure the lights are functioning. They should remain lighted from sunset until midnight, but check with your representative for exact hours in your area.

Have your Outdoor Billboard Worksheet filled out by your reps when you are ready to think about outdoor advertising. Among other things, it will provide a list of available locations which would be appropriate for servicing your business. Because different board locations become available at various times throughout the year, plan as early as possible to ensure the best locations (with the exceptions discussed in the following "Contracts" section).

The completed Outdoor Worksheets will let you know at a glance when your contract date starts and ends, and most importantly, when you need to notify the outdoor company to avoid an *automatic renewal* of your contract. The automatic renewal clause is covered in the next section.

Contracts: You will have the opportunity to work with your outdoor rep(s) to customize contracts for your particular budget. As with radio and television, you should discuss discounts for any long term contracts — meaning 13 weeks or more. When committing yourself for a lengthy period, you should know that outdoor billboard companies are among the toughest for allowing a contract cancellation.

- Painted units are non-cancelable. The up-front investment to the outdoor company is high and recaptured gradually over the life of the contract.

- Long term contracts can pose a problem if you want to cancel half-way through. Before signing a long-term contract be sure you can afford it and look for a cancellation clause if you are concerned with finances.

  The advantage of planning ahead and signing a long-term contract is having the ability to secure the best board locations. But it would be wiser to take your chances on choosing from whatever boards are available closer to the time you want to advertise, and buy one month at a time if you foresee any problem with long-term financing.

- For submission purposes, put different co-op products on separate contracts.

  Be sure to submit your claims within the specified time limits (usually 45-60 days) with all of the appropriate paperwork. If no co-op program is readily available, contact your largest distributors to see if one can be implemented.

  You will need prior approval on any art work that is not directly provided by your distributor.

- Look for an automatic renewal clause in your contract! It means that even though there is an end date on your contract, it will be automatically renewed unless you notify the company in writing of your desire not to renew. And you may have to give the written non-renewal as much as 90 days in advance of your contract end date.

Tip: When the contracts on your board(s) expire, your outdoor company will probably leave your designs up until the locations are sold to someone else.

Bulletins:
These large illu-
minated boards
deliver impact in
size, placement,
color and light-

ing. They can measure 10'6" x 32' or 14' x 48'
and larger. You'll find these along major highways.

30-Sheet Posters: These
boards, placed along smaller
roads and some highways,
deliver your message to res-
idents and incoming travelers. These panels measure 12 feet

high by 24 feet wide with an actual design area of 9'7" x 21'7" (plus blank paper
borders).

8-Sheet Posters: These panels, measuring
6 feet in height by 12 feet wide, with a
design area of 5' x 11', do the same job at a
lower price and work well for 40 MPH and
under — generally in the heart of most towns and
cities.

Outdoor Billboard Worksheet

Company Name: __ABC Outdoor__   Rep's Name: _____Jeff Doe_____

Phone Number: __555-1111__   Fax Number: _____555-1112_____

Board Size	Paint/Paper/Vinyl	Location	Monthly Rent	Date Available
30-sheet	_____	690W	$ 1,500	6/1/98
30-sheet	paper	X.1st St.	$ 750	6/15/98
_____	_____	_____	$ _____	_____
_____	_____	_____	$ _____	_____
_____	_____	_____	$ _____	_____
_____	_____	_____	$ _____	_____

Production cost: $ __1,250__ every # __45__ days. Contract dates: __6/1__ to __7/31__

Does contract have an automatic renewal clause?   Yes _____   No __X__

Date of notification due: _____   In writing: Yes _____   No __X__

Co-op being used?   Yes _____   No __X__   What brand? _____

Special Instructions: __Blue with white lettering__

_____

Sample Art Work

Multiple Boards

Board Number	Location	Up date	Down date	Production $	Monthly rent
348	690W	6/1	7/31	$1,000	$1,500
315	8IN	6/1	6/30	$750	$1,000
613	695	6/1	7/31	$1,000	$1,500

Transit Advertising

Transit advertising adds mobility to outdoor billboards. At one time, advertisers tended to shy away from transit advertising because of the perception of who the bus rider might be. Was the desired audience the person who could not afford a car? Today, concern for the environment and the popularity of programs such as Park-and-Ride, have a wide range of business professionals, teachers, college students and many other types of workers, leaving their cars in mall parking lots and riding the bus to and from their jobs. It saves them the often high cost of parking, the wear-and-tear on the cars, and provides them the opportunity to review material for a morning meeting, study, or just relax and gather their thoughts for the busy day ahead.

Not only can you reach some very upscale customers on the inside of the bus, but you can also reach a large variety of people by advertising on the more traditional, more popular exterior signs on buses. Available in various shapes and sizes, exterior bus signs display advertising messages on both city and suburban buses. Each day they pass by thousands of people in cars, as well as pedestrians. Buses travel through cities and outlying suburban areas, to shopping malls, universities, business districts, amusement centers, supermarkets, theaters, and convention sites. Local customers, as well as visitors to your area, will be exposed to your large moving messages.

When considering your design, treat the signs as moving outdoor billboards. People won't have a chance to look at the message for a long period of time, so use bright colors to attract attention, and simple ideas with just a few words for effective transit advertising.

In the last few years it has become very popular to "wrap" an entire bus with the theme of a company, a product, a museum, even camouflage wrap for an army recruiting campaign. These giant moving advertisements are impossible to miss and are a lot of fun to look at. Wrapping a bus is an expensive proposition, and you will generally be required to sign a contract that will keep you paying "rent" on your bus for a minimum of one year. But if you have the budget, and your company or product lends itself to the size and shape of a bus, you can get a lot of mileage (no pun intended) from this form of advertising. Discounts are available for buying multiple signs and for multiple-month contracts.

Whether you advertise in, on or over the whole bus, you can request that your bus travels on very specific routes or, if your message has broad audience appeal, on a bus that travels many routes to cover your maximum desired audience throughout your contract period. Your bus company will provide you with a complete list of routes.

If you plan on being a regular transit advertiser, speak to the Director of Marketing at the bus company about placing an ad in the next batch of schedules they print. Schedules are usually updated annually, so use a generic ad that won't become outdated over that period of time.

The following photos are examples of wrapped buses in Syracuse, NY:

Photo courtesy of Kraft Foods, Inc.

Photo courtesy of C.N.Y. Centro, Inc.

Photo courtesy of Everson Museum, Syracuse, NY.

Photo courtesy of Cellular One, Syracuse, NY.

Remember these ads from the Outdoor Advertising section? This television station used the same ads on buses. When the initial teaser ads were on long enough, they completed the signs with individuals from the original billboard artwork, rather than the whole group of people.

Photos courtesy of WIXT-TV, Syracuse, NY.

Outdoor billboards and transit signs are very effective when used together as in the photos below. The combination keeps some of your signs anchored and some mobile for great coverage.

Photos courtesy of WIXT-TV, Syracuse, NY.

Transit Worksheet #1

**Have your transit rep fill out this worksheet for your general information.
Use Worksheet #2 when you are actually ready to use this form of advertising.**

Company Name: _ABC Transit_   Phone Number: _555-6666_

Account Executive: _____   Fax Number: _555-6667_

Monthly Rent Per Bus

King size: $ _140_   Queen size: $ _140_   Traveling Displays: $ _50_

Headlight signs: $ _80_   Tail signs: $ _100_   Driver signs: $ _10_

Bus wraps: $ _1,500_   Discounts available: _52 wk = 10% discount_

Production Cost

King size: $ _450_   Queen size: $ _450_   Traveling Displays: $ _140_

Headlight signs: $ _140_   Tail signs: $ _175_   Driver signs: $ _110_

Bus wraps: $ _1,200_   Discounts available: _1_

Side panel signs

| King – 30" x 144" | Queen – 30" x 88" |

Headlight signs

21" x 40"

Tail signs (top and bottom)

21" x 70"

Traveling display signs

21" x 44"

Interior signs

11" x 28"

Behind driver signs

14" x 19"

Transit Worksheet #2

Have your transit rep complete this worksheet when you are ready to advertise.

Company Name:_____   Phone Number: _____

Account Executive: _____   Fax Number: _____

Dates to schedule: _____ to _____ Number of weeks: _____

Total number of exterior signs: _____ Total number of interior signs: _____

# of King size: _____ # of Queen size:_____ # of Traveling Displays: _____

# of Headlight signs: _____ # of Tail signs:_____ # of Driver signs: _____

Campaign title:_____ Discount: _____

Production cost:$ _____ Rent per month:$_____ Total contract cost:$ _____

Specific routes: _____

_____

❑   Please check here to request rotation of bus(s) through all available routes.

Side panel signs

King – 30" x 144"	Queen – 30" x 88"

Headlight signs

21" x 40"

Tail signs (top and bottom)

21" x 70"

Traveling display signs

21" x 44"

Interior signs

11" x 28"

Behind driver signs

14" x 19"

10

Kiss It Goodnight, and Put It to Bed

The term "put it to bed" means wrap it up and tie all of the loose ends together. There are a few loose ends I would like to tie up for you.

Using the Internet

Since the early 1990s, the Internet has been a viable avenue for advertising. Advertising on the "Net" originally consisted of World Wide Web ("WWW" or "the Web") sites by computer software and hardware manufacturers who saw the Internet as a new way of providing technical support and customer assistance. This gave the consumer access to a wealth of information about the manufacturer's product 24 hours a day, whenever the consumer wanted or needed it. Anyone who has recently needed to connect to a computer company's web site to obtain the latest update for some critical piece of software can attest to the Internet's usefulness as a support medium.

Soon after the computer companies were "on-line," many other non-computer-oriented corporations joined the crowd. At the start, corporate sites were nothing more than logo showcases which slowly grew to include other amenities, such as merchandise decorated with the company logos. Today, serious Internet advertising continues to increase via the World Wide Web (any address starting with "http:" or "www").

Your computer can become an important source of information for opening, operating, and growing a successful small business. There is so much material on the Internet, you could never hope to access all of it. But you can quickly check out web addresses you find in interesting business magazine articles and business-related television programs for a bit of relevant information you might otherwise not stumble upon. Because these web sites change frequently and often disappear altogether, there is not a current list for me to recommend.

Most of the addresses I might list for your use today would no longer exist by the time you read this book.

The Small Business Administration's web site is an exception (http://www.sba.gov), and should be continually available. It will provide you with a wealth of information on many topics such as how to start a home-based business, where to find start-up financing, incubator programs, counseling, exporting, conferences, training programs, and the addresses, phone numbers, and fax numbers of local Small Business Administration offices all over the United States. Links from this site also provide toll-free numbers to SBA services, programs, trade fairs, seminars, and marketing advice.

Along with accessing this type of functional information, you may also wish to introduce the world to your business via electronic mail order and attract customers and clients no matter how far away they may be. For that, you (or someone else) must design a basic business web site.

Most companies use an Internet Service Provider, or ISP, to take care of setting up the web site's connection to the outside world, securing your domain name (name of your web site), and keeping your Internet connection running. Three ISP examples are America Online (www.aol.com), IBM Global Network (www.ibm.net), and CompuServe (www.compuserve.com).

Before developing the actual web site, you will have to do some advance preparation. You must pre-determine what the format of your web site will be, how much and what text it will contain, whether or not you will use graphics or music in your presentation, and how many pages the site will hold, to name just a few of the details. You will even have to estimate how many "hits" or visits you might expect your web site to receive. This information will, in part, determine the cost of your site's connection to the Internet. And you will need to update the information periodically to keep it current and interesting to those who may visit more than once or twice.

If you are not a computer expert, or you don't have the time or inclination to even search out software to help you design the pages of a web site, contact your local SBA office or Chamber of Commerce and ask if they can recommend someone who creates web sites for a living. You may find a fellow entrepreneur who is just getting started and will give you a good price in exchange for recommending him or her to others.

Getting on the Internet with a web site may not be your top priority when opening a new business, but keep it in mind. At the very least you can use the Internet as an invaluable research tool. Check out the web sites of your competitors to see what they're up to! Before long, you will probably find yourself being dragged (some of you kicking and screaming) into the 21st century with a business web site!

Tip: Keep the text portions of your web page(s) short. No one wants to read and read and read a web page. Use color, graphics, even music, to keep the page(s) interesting and the reader reading.

Responsibilities of a Good Advertiser

There are many ways you can help your reps do their jobs well — none of which take a lot of time or money.

Giving your media reps plenty of notice of upcoming advertising is one of the most important responsibilities — not only to them — but to you. Last minute advertising is like last minute Christmas shopping. You end up getting things you're not really happy with and you usually pay too much to get them. In the end, nobody wins. You're unhappy because the advertising did not create the response you'd hoped it would and the rep is unhappy because you'll be less likely to call him again.

Every kind of media has a deadline — and they're all different. Of all the types of media you can buy, radio is the one you can deal with the fastest as far as producing commercials, or starting a schedule within a day, as long as the station has the inventory available. You can move almost as quickly with television if you already have a commercial produced and it happens to already be at the station you call. Print deadlines can vary from three to four days before publication for small papers to a week before publication with larger papers and sometimes 10 days to 2 weeks for special sections.

You will be happier with your ads and the results they spark if you work ahead of time with each of your reps to give them a chance to think things through, look for upcoming special opportunities that correspond with your time requirements, and put extra effort into tying in copy and coordinating the layout and design of your print ads with your other media.

One of the most counterproductive things you can do as an advertiser is to give false feedback to your media salespeople. When your rep(s) ask you how the advertising worked, give totally accurate answers. If it worked, say so — and also say so if it didn't work at all. If you tell a rep that your advertising did not work when it did, he or she will change what was done for the next schedule. Clients sometimes think if they indicate that the advertising did not work well, the rep will work harder the next time. In reality, it makes the rep change a schedule that worked well to something that may not work at all the next time.

During one of my years as a radio sales rep I was told that a client, who was running a "pick your own strawberries" ad, had called the station to cancel the remainder of his schedule because there were so many people in the field they were trampling the strawberries. When a new rep from the station was assigned to that client a few weeks later, the first question he asked was "How did the last schedule work for you?" The client shrugged his shoulders and said, "OK."

The client now had a radio rep who was going to work very hard to change the schedule *that worked so well it had to be canceled* (one of the catch-22 situations radio sales reps face). Not only is this unfair to the radio rep who will waste precious time and energy trying to figure out what went wrong, but when the new, altered schedule doesn't work, the rep will feel that he or she has let the client down and question his/her own ability. It's a bad scene all the way around. So please give credit when credit is due and, of course, be honest as well when the schedule doesn't work.

And Here's a Big One!

Pay those invoices on time. There is a grapevine large enough to choke a horse in the world of advertising. Everyone knows who pays on time and who doesn't. Monthly collection meetings are held within every media sales department to discuss clients who are behind in their payments. And all reps have friends within the business. They know who pays within 30 days and who is way out there. You won't be able to negotiate your next advertising schedule from a position of strength, and you don't want to go back to the days of being asked to pay cash-in-advance — especially after you've worked hard to reach the point where you can call in a schedule and have it happily taken over the phone.

You will generally be given some slack on the portion of your bill being paid by *co-op*. Co-op is the part of your advertising being paid by a supplier of brand name products you carry or by your franchise company. It's been around long enough that people know it takes a while for it to come in. You will need to fork over your percent within 30 days, but generally you will not be asked to pay the co-op portion before it is received by you.

Watch Out!

There are many advertising rules and regulations you must strictly adhere to. You cannot advertise a "Going out of business" sale if you are not actually going out of business. You cannot advertise items at a low price when you don't have the items in stock or use the ad to sell higher priced merchandise (called "Bait and Switch" advertising). Don't take a chance. Call the Federal Trade Commission (FTC) for rules and regulations if you don't know them.

You also have a responsibility to yourself and the enterprise you have undertaken to constantly think of new and creative ways to promote your business. If your business would lend itself to sharing advertising with someone else, don't be afraid to approach another business owner.

For instance, a garden shop could easily team up with a store selling patio and lawn furniture. The garden shop would leave coupons for a percentage off of trees and shrubs at the furniture store, and the furniture store would leave coupons at the garden store for a percent off patio and lawn furniture. Your radio, television, and print ads would include both businesses — and you would split the cost of production and advertising. Choose businesses in the same general vicinity to maximize the chances of customers visiting both places. In cases like this it is best to put the money in up front to avoid the possibility of one or the other business paying his/her half late.

That same lawn and garden shop could team up with a swimming pool company. Or the pool company could team up with the summer furniture company — there can be more than one great match for your business. Picture the person who may buy your product or use your service. Imagine what a typical day of your client or customer might be. You will be surprised at the number of combinations you will come up with for shared advertising opportunities in your community!

A client of mine recently added a large water park to his outdoor family entertainment complex called Thunder Island. The water slides were finished in time

for the last part of the summer, but there was no time to landscape. Because installing the water park had been so expensive, I thought it would be a great idea to find a way to provide the landscaping for my client at little or no cost with the help of local professional landscape companies. But to work, the plan had to be worthwhile for all parties involved.

I sent the letter on page 110 with a photo of the areas in need of landscaping and some free All-Day Water Park Passes to local landscape companies. The free passes allowed them to see and use the water slides, and

Would You Trade Plants For Wet Pants?

Thunder Island in Fulton has just opened a brand new Water Park for people of all ages.

Now it needs to be landscaped.

Following in the tradition of other great theme parks, Thunder Island would like to invite local landscape professionals to each choose a small section of the Water Park area to landscape as "Photo Op Spots." You are free to use end-of-the-year nursery stock and bulbs you have available to you in the fall to create your own signature space. Planting areas must be "finished" with mulch, pebbles, or ground cover that will keep the areas as weed-free as possible.

Thunder Island will provide permanent identity signs or plaques to be installed in your landscaped area with the name and location of your business.

You will also receive 100 All-Day Water Park Passes for the 1998 season to be used for your family, friends, or customers, a $900 value, and be included in the resulting press release program.

We hope you are able to participate in this "Photo Op Spot" program. Then, provide your family, friends and customers with 100 passes to "wet their pants" at the new Water Park. Thousands of people from all over Central New York will see your landscaped area and the name of your business year after year. In the meantime, please enjoy the enclosed 1997 Water Park Passes any day in August or on a weekend in September.

Please call me at (315) 487-6706 and I will arrange to meet you at Thunder Island located in Fulton (Wilcox Rd. & Rte. 48) to show you the areas to choose from. Thank you for your time and consideration.

Sincerely,

Kathy J. Kobliski

President/Silent Partner Advertising/Thunder Island Agency of Record/August 18, 1997
(315) 487-6706

to choose the section that most attracted them. We provided figures on the number of people who used the park before the water slides were installed and the estimated number of people who would frequent the park as a result of the addition.

Within two weeks, most of the sections to be landscaped had been claimed by local professional landscapers who saw this project for what it was — a great opportunity to take advantage of a marketing program that would provide them with advertising to thousands of people for years to come at a one-time investment of their inventory and work. Since most of the work could not be done until the park was closed for the season, the landscapers were also able to use end-of-the-year inventory, and do the planting during their "off-season."

Advantages to the Landscapers

• The landscape companies have the opportunity for thousands of people see their work first hand, and they are able to provide their customers with the "value added" aspect to purchases — free water slide passes.

Advantages to Thunder Island

• The Water Park gets landscaped at no cost to the owner, and the landscape companies become distribution points for passes to the park.

"Everybody wins" must be at the very core of every plan when more than one business is combining efforts for a common goal — promotional value for all — equally. Give a lot of thought to the project before you approach your would-be partner(s). Make a list of possible advantages to all parties, then put yourself in the place of each participant and decide if you would be happy with the advantages they are slated to receive. Remember that each participant may have different advantages, but they must be equal in perceived value.

Once you have your plan, start contacting prospective partners in your area. You can do it by phone or by mail with a promotional piece as I did.

Don't be afraid of rejection. You will find that many small businesses are anxious to hear about creative, cooperative plans to promote their business. You can make projects like this happen for your business.

List some businesses that might be interested in sharing a promotional project with you:

_____

_____

Check Your Invoices

When your invoices arrive at the end of each broadcast month, check them over thoroughly to be sure they correspond exactly with your original contracts. Make sure that the correct number of commercials or print ads ran, that they ran on the correct days and within the specified ranges of times. If you find any discrepancies, do not pay for the errant charges. Just subtract them from the total bill and let your rep know what you're doing and why. For instance, a typical radio contract might look like this:

	Monday	Tuesday	Wednesday	Thursday	Friday	Saturday
6 AM – 10 AM	1X	2X	2X	3X	2X	
10 AM – 3 PM	1X	1X	1X	1X	1X	1X
3 PM – 7 PM	1X	1X	1X	2X	2X	1X

This schedule represents 24 commercials to run in very specific dayparts over a six-day period. If the invoice comes in showing that one commercial ran at 5:25 AM (before the 6 AM start time) and one ran at 7:30 PM (after the 7 PM end time), those two commercials need not be paid for. If 23 of the spots ran correctly, but one ran on Sunday, which is not a contracted day, the Sunday spot would be deducted from the bill.

This is something you need to do with every invoice. Most often, your rep will know that this has happened to your schedule. If the traffic department of a radio or television station needs to move a spot, they will tell the rep and in turn, the rep will alert you to see what you want to do. Move the spot? Cancel the spot? It's up to you. However, now and then something will happen to a schedule without the rep's knowledge. You are the final examiner of paperwork, and since it's your money, don't overlook the step.

If your print ad runs with the wrong colors, the wrong lay-out, or deviates from your instructions, ask for a make-good. If one can't be given in time for your sale or event, get the charge eliminated. Print reps might ask you to consider whether the ad had any value at all, even though it wasn't 100 percent the way you wanted it. This is an attempt to get you to pay a percent of the bill rather than not pay at all.

Ask him or her this question: If the guests at your daughter's wedding were supposed to be fed prime rib and shrimp at the reception, but were fed baked chicken and potato salad instead, would you pay for the meal? The caterer could argue that there was some value to the meal because it was eaten by the wedding guests — it served a purpose. I can guarantee you that they would not pay for the meal. The menu was chosen specifically to match the atmosphere of the wedding, the character of the family, and as a thank you to the guests who attended and brought gifts. Chicken would not fill the bill when prime rib was intended.

The look of your print ad — the colors, the design, the copy, etc. must create a feeling, a look, and provide an impression of your company. You put a lot of thought, work, and money into getting it just right and running it at just the right time. Make sure it's what you intended. Don't pay for chicken when you ordered prime rib.

Keeping 15 Percent

If you are a large enough advertiser, the media may accept you as an in-house agency if you can meet a few requirements. Usually when you do this a station or publication will ask if you handle any other clients. Your answer to this is "No, it's an in-house agency, meaning we represent only ourselves."

An in-house agency has certain responsibilities such as providing finished scripts for radio and television commercials and giving specific instructions to your print reps on how you want your ad to look. While regular advertising agencies provide camera-ready art work for print ads and already-produced radio and television commercials to radio and television stations, an in-house agency can usually get away with written scripts and sketched artwork. You will find that while most forms of media recognize formal advertising agencies (and many in-house agencies) as a matter of routine, many newspapers do not recognize either kind. A gross total on a contract includes a 15 percent commission, while a net total does not. Check each contract you sign.

The small print on many contracts states that agencies are responsible for delivering finished radio and television spots to the station(s) two or three days in advance of schedules rather than asking the reps to pick them up. But generally, reps provide pick-ups from agencies as a normal function of daily business. An advertising agency does not rely on the help of rep(s) for deciding how heavy a schedule to run or what the placement should be, as a direct advertiser would. In order for a media business to grant you in-house status, you will have to be a regular advertiser who spends in the neighborhood of $40 to $50 thousand a year. Small business owners do not normally have a large enough budget to worry about saving 15 percent at the risk of losing the talent and support always available from reps to direct advertisers. But for those direct advertisers who have a nice fat budget to back them up and the time to do the extra work or an employee designated to handle it for them, it's possible to save 15 percent of the advertising budget.

There are different percents of annual budgets allotted for advertising. When you first go into business start with an amount — 10 percent of your budget is not unheard of — designated for your first year's advertising ventures. Then at the end of your first year, figure 3–5 percent of the gross receipts and plan to use that amount for your second year.

A common trap direct advertisers often fall into occurs when they "back into" the process of determining the percent of advertising expenditures against their profits. Business owners have said to me, "I use 10 percent as an advertising figure. Therefore, if I spend $500 in advertising, I need to recover $5,000 in business to justify spending the $500 in the first place." That's working backwards — it's the wrong way to do it — and it will drive you crazy! Your first advertising figure is an amount you set aside as a portion of your entire operating budget. After that, as I mentioned before, you use a percent of your gross total receipts from year one for the second year's advertising budget.

Just as I can promise that your incoming mail will triple after you open your business doors, I can tell you that each and every year your accountant will tell you that you spend too much money on advertising and will recommend you reduce it to improve the bottom line. Tell him/her about that wink in the dark and ask for suggestions on how you can otherwise motivate customers to line up in front of your cash register. Hopefully you can make the point that without advertising you are winking in the dark! And, if along the way you can qualify as an in-house agency, your accountant will smile right along with you at the prospect of saving 15 percent!

Tracking Results

There was once a nun who spent her entire adult life wondering what it must have been like for the Virgin Mary to have lived life with Jesus as a boy. She excitedly anticipated her own death, thinking of it as the long awaited opportunity to ask the Virgin Mary the question and to at long last hear the answer. Finally, the nun passed away. The first thing she did in Heaven was find Mary. Almost unable to contain the excitement of hearing the answer to her question, she blurted out, "Tell me, Blessed Mother, what was it like living with Jesus as a boy?" Mary thought for a moment and then replied, " To tell you the truth, I had been hoping for a girl."

We don't always get the end result that makes us happy. Sometimes sales or promotions don't work out as we had hoped. Remember that the demographic numbers we use can only serve as a guide. There is no 100 percent guarantee that every advertising campaign will work. But if you have placed your advertising dollars properly, the advertising will not be wasted. Even though your audience may not respond to the specifics of a certain campaign, it has heard your business name, your location, and is getting familiar with what you do there.

One of the hardest things to do is accurately track and analyze the results of your advertising. We do know that mail-back offers and coupons are easily tracked. But how do you track other kinds of advertising?

For businesses carrying a variety of inventory, it is possible to follow the sale of individual items or brands advertised on different radio and television stations. For instance, the wallpaper department of a decorating outlet may be advertised on one particular radio station while the furniture or carpet department may be advertised solely on a second radio station — or on television. And that same store might advertise a paint sale in print or with coupons in direct mail. The items showing a definite increase in business during and immediately following the advertising (memory will only last two weeks after the advertising stops) will tell you which stations, print ads, or coupons are working and which are not.

If you fill out a Tracking Results Worksheet for each campaign, you will see a pattern of how much money you spent, where you spent it, and what kind of results you experienced. If you advertise the same sale, product, or event in several forms of media in one campaign, you will know that the whole campaign worked or did not work, but you may not have a clear indication of which part worked the best. In this instance, don't worry too much. An overall success is always good news and as you keep track of campaign after campaign, you will recognize how best to disperse your advertising funds.

The Annual Tracking Worksheet will tell you how much you actually spent during a 52 week period, and where you spent it. Your advertising year does not have to start in January. It can start whenever you begin keeping track of your advertising on these worksheets, as long as you maintain the information for 52 consecutive weeks. Many businesses I have worked with have annual budgets that start in the month of March or June. Your annual budget starts when you are ready to advertise, or at least ready to keep track of your advertising dollars.

If you have taken the time to fill out the Tracking Worksheet for each campaign, add up the amounts spent on each medium and each vehicle within them (specific stations and publication, etc.). You will see if you placed the bulk of your advertising into one particular form of media or if you distributed the funds evenly into many forms.

Both tracking sheets are important to have with you when you negotiate future advertising rates. If you have kept accurate records, there will be no question as

Tracking Results Worksheet

Dates of campaign: __6/1/98__ to __6/ /98__ Total budget $ __9,945.00__

Media used: ❏ Radio ❏ Television ❏ Print ❏ Direct Mail ❏ Outdoor

Radio stations and number of spots on each: __WZAQ (24X), WQAZ (24X)__

__WOOO (24X)__ Production/talent cost: $ __none__

Length of radio spots ☒ 60 second spots ❏ 30 second spots

Total cost of radio: $ __5,470.00__

Television stations and number of spots on each: __Channel 6 (12X), Channel 8 (12X)__

_____ Production/talent cost: $ __675.00__

Length of television spots ❏ 10 second spots ☒ 30 second spots ❏ 60 second spots

Total cost of television: $ __3,000.00__

Print/Publication(s) used: __Daily Paper__

Date of publication: __6/3/98__ Second date: __6/4/98__

Size of ad: __1/4 page__ Size of second ad: __1/4 page__

Total cost of print: $ __800.00__

Number of direct mail pieces: __none__

❏ Mailed

Date mailed: _____ Second mailing: _____

❏ Inserts

Publication used: _____

Date: _____ Second date: _____

Total cost of direct mail: $ _____

Outdoor billboards/company name: __none__

Number of boards: _____ Size of boards: _____

Location of boards: _____

Total cost of outdoor: $ _____

The campaign had: ❏ No results ❏ Some results ☒ Good results ❏ Great results

Notes: __Used clambake Friday copy__

_____

**Attach copies of radio and television scripts, print ads, and coupons to this sheet for future reference.

Annual Tracking Worksheet

Year: __1/1/97__ to __12/31/97__ Total budget $ _____

Media used: ☒ Radio ☒ Television ❑ Print ❑ Direct Mail ☒ Outdoor ❑Transit

Radio: Station/Total Amount/Discount %

WZAQ	19,000	5%
WQAZ	12,000	5%
WOOO	30,000	10%

Radio Grand Total: $ __61,000__

Television: Station/Total Amount/Discount %

Channel 6	10,500	5%
Channel 3	3,020	—
Channel 2	8,000	—
Channel 3	12,400	5%

Television Grand Total: $ __33,920__

Print: Publication Daily/Weekly Discount % Total Amount

Print Grand Total: $ _____

Outdoor Billboards: Total Amount (rent and production)

$9,750	7,000	+	2,750
$3,250	2,000	+	1,250

Outdoor Grand Total: $ __13,000__

Direct Mail: Type Total Amount (coupons, brochures,etc.)

Direct Mail Grand Total: $ _____

Transit: Total Amount Total # of Signs (exterior + interior) Total # of Wraps

Transit Grand Total: $ _____

Co-op: _____ **Brands Used:** __none__ **Total Amount:** _____

Total Co-op Dollars Captured: $ _____

to how much you paid per spot or per column inch, what discount you received, or what you paid for production.

Remember to ask all of your reps to update the radio, television, print, direct mail, and outdoor advertising worksheets as rates officially change.

Once you get used to working from your worksheets you will be able to make the right decisions quickly, and save yourself enormous amounts of time and money to boot. You will spend less of your own personal time on advertising because your reps will be doing the work. And that's good — because you have a thousand other things to do every day!

Tip: Plan your advertising. Last minute advertising is like last minute Christmas shopping. You end up paying too much money and you're not really happy with what you buy.

Set Up a Binder

The media worksheets in this book, when completed by your media reps, will provide critical standardized information free of "fluff" and irrelevant facts. Setting up a binder of these worksheets would organize your information and save lots of time when you decide it's time to advertise. Use a 2½" binder and a set of eight dividers. Label the dividers in the following manner:

• Customer Information
• Radio
• Television
• Print
• Direct Mail
• Outdoor
• Tracking Results
• Media Forms

Copy the media worksheets onto three-ring paper and give them to the appropriate Account Executives. When you get the completed worksheets back, put them in the corresponding section for easy access. Also copy the Customer Information and Tracking Worksheets on three-ring paper. The binder will keep this information together and available when it's time to assess the data.

Let There Be Light ...

Things don't happen like that in advertising. It takes a while to establish your business name. It's like pushing a ball uphill. You have to keep going because if you stop pushing, the ball rolls back down the hill and you have to start all over. There is a snowball effect that occurs with your advertising efforts, each schedule building upon whatever impact the previous schedule made. The absolute wrong thing to do is to start advertising and then disappear for a while. You must make a commitment to it and have the strength to see it through.

Any form of advertising will work if used correctly. That's why you see ads for radio stations on bus signs, television ads in the newspaper, and commercials for your local transit company on the radio. They all use *each other* — this tells you emphatically that no one form of advertising can be expected to do it all for any business.

That doesn't mean that you shouldn't adjust what you're doing when things don't seem to be working, or try different kinds of advertising to see what works best for you. Remember that all advertising will work if you use it correctly. And I can't stress that enough. Sticking your big toe in will never be enough. You can't "try" advertising. You have to use advertising. It takes guts to wait for results while you watch money rolling out. That's why you need the information in this book. You will still need the guts, but you will be confident that the money you spend will not be wasted. And that means you won't have to wait as long for the results.

Small business owners are among my very favorite people. They are gutsy, energetic, hopeful, and brave. Each entrepreneur has that mysterious incentive that drives him or her to believe that almost anything is possible. Good luck to each of you in your endeavors.

Feel free to e-mail me at Media106@aol.com with your ideas for topic expansions or additions for future editions.

Tip: If you have a web site, save on your newspaper ads by buying classified ads with an interesting heading and your web site address. Example:

Kitchen Remodeling from $300!

www.KitchenDeal.com.

You can give lots of details, photos, and even list testimonials on your web site.

Glossary

Adjacency. A commercial placed right next to a special feature such as weather, news, sports, or traffic reports.

Affidavit. Notarized invoices showing specific days and times commercials ran. All co-op invoices and scripts must be notarized for submission purposes.

Afternoon Drive. The 3 PM – 7 PM section of a radio day or daypart.

Announcement. Commercial message of varying lengths on radio or television.

Annual Discount. Rate discount applied to contracts of 52 continuous week duration.

Arbitron. Television and radio rating service measuring listening/viewing audiences.

Audience Composition. Demographic makeup of a group of people represented in an audience grouped by age, gender, etc.

Automatic Renewal. A clause sometimes found in Outdoor Advertising contracts indicating the need to cancel contracts (in writing) 90 days in advance to avoid the automatic renewal of the contract.

Billboard. (Radio) An ID announcement of a program or feature sponsor.

Billboard. (Outdoor) Painted, printed or poster advertising boards along roads and highways.

Brochure. Printed promotional piece available in many sizes.

Cable. Television signals transmitted by wire, or cable, instead of through the air. Cable television provides the availability of programming from more and distant stations for a monthly fee.

Cancellation Date. A specific, published date for canceling an advertising contract.

Cash Discount. A deduction sometimes passed on to advertisers for payment of invoices within a short period of time — usually 15 days.

Circulation. (Print) Number of copies sold or delivered.

Circulation. (Outdoor) Number of people who drive by a given board location within a 24 hour period.

Column Inch. A newspaper measurement of the smallest possible ad — one column wide by one inch long.

Co-op Advertising. The shared cost of advertising between an advertiser and a manufacturer.

Copy. The written script for radio or television spots or the word section of a print ad.

Coupon(ing). Distribution of coupons through the mail, print, or in-store promotion.

Coverage Map. Diagram showing a medium's geographical audience potential.

Daypart. A specific segment of a broadcast day.

Demographics. Segments of population grouped by age and gender.

Direct Mail. Print pieces sent through the mail to consumers.

Drive Time. Morning and afternoon radio dayparts (5:30 - 10 AM and 3 - 7 PM).

Dub. A copy of a radio or television commercial.

Exclusivity. Advertising at a given period of time free from competing ads.

Fixed Rate. Cost of spots running at the same time every day.

Flat Rate. Advertising rate before discounts.

Frequency. Average number of times a person is exposed to a commercial message.

Frequency Discount. Discount given for reaching a specific number of commercials of print, radio, television, or outdoor ads per week, month, or year.

Flight. A short radio or television schedule.

Font. Style of lettering.

HUT. (Households using television) Nielsen term for audience determination.

In-House Agency. The term given to an advertiser who independently plans and places media schedules, provides his/her own produced commercials and print ads, and receives a 15 percent commission for doing so.

Insert. A printed piece delivered to consumers inside of a daily or weekly newspaper.

Makegood. A commercial run as a replacement for one missed or pre-exempted from a regular schedule on radio, television, or in print.

Nielsen. A.C. Nielsen Company — national television rating service.

Primary Audience. A station's largest demographic segment of viewers or listeners.

Promotion. A heightened form of advertising including special extra features.

Psychographics. Data sometimes used along with demographics to identify a group of people by education, income, hobbies, credit habits, etc.

Pulsing. Advertising technique of scheduling alternating periods of advertising and periods of non-advertising.(Example: One week off, one week on).

PUT. (Persons Using Television) Nielsen term for audience determination.

Rate Card. A published list of rates, deadlines, cancellation specifications, for all media.

Rating. The audience shown as a percent of the total population.

Reach. The number of different persons or households exposed to a commercial message.

Remnant Space. Radio, television, or print space sold at reduced rates.

Remote. Broadcasting a radio or television show from an outside location.

Rotary Program. Moving a number of outdoor billboards to different locations over a period of time.

Shared Advertising. An advertising campaign featuring the sharing of commercial production and cost by two or more advertisers.

Shopper. A local, weekly newspaper usually delivered to homes at no cost.

Showing. A group of outdoor billboards up at one time in various locations.

Sponsorship. The purchase by one advertiser of a specific station feature such as weather, sports, news, or traffic reports.

Spot. One commercial on radio or television.

Strategic Advertising. (Also called "maintenance" advertising.) Running a small schedule over a long period of time.

Sweeps. Both Arbitron and Nielsen survey all television local markets four times per year (November, February, May, and July).

Tabloid. A smaller than standard-sized newspaper or special newspaper section.

Tactical Advertising. Running a large amount of commercials in a short period of time.

TAP. (Total audience plan) — Radio schedule made up of all dayparts at a reasonable rate.

Target Audience. A specific group of people defined by age and gender by an advertiser.

Tear Sheet. An actual page containing the advertising being invoiced as proof of publication.

Vehicle. A specific station or publication within a general media classification.

Volume Discount. A rate discount given for running a specific (large) number of radio, television, or print ads within a given contract.

Worksheets

Some of the sample worksheets and forms throughout the book were partially completed to show how they will look after use, and what kinds of information you can expect them to provide.

This section includes clean copies of all those worksheets and forms for you to tear out, duplicate, and use. As suggested in Chapter 10, the most effective employment of them would be to copy them onto three-ring paper and keep them in a binder. Structure in this area of your business is critical to taking control of advertising expenditures. Following instructions and organizing your completed paperwork once will save you time and keep your advertising budget under control — meaning your dollars are placed where they work the hardest. The initial numbers of each sheet to print and place in your binder are as follows:

Worksheet Type	Number of Copies	Appropriate Section
Customer Information	10	Customer Information
Radio (3)	10 of each	Radio Section
Television	10	Television Section
Print	10	Print Section
Direct Mail	10	Direct Mail Section
Outdoor Advertising (2)	5 of each	Outdoor Section
Transit (2)	4 of each	Outdoor Section
Tracking	10	Tracking Results
Annual Tracking	4	Tracking Results

Forms

:30 Second Script Sheets	10	Media Forms
:60 Second Script Sheets	10	Media Forms
Consent and Release	10	Media Forms

Customer Information Worksheet

Dates: _____ to _____

Zip Codes	Gender	Age (estimate)

Zip Codes	Gender	Age	
_____	Females _____	12–24	_____
_____	_____	25–35	_____
_____	Males _____	36–50	_____
_____	_____	over 50	_____

Consent and Release Form

With my signature below, I consent to the use of my name, voice, or image for the following:

Business Name: _____

Title of spot or ad: _____

Dates ad will run: _____ to _____

❏   Check this box for unlimited use.

❏   I have read and understand this form.

❏   I am 18 years old.

❏   I am the minor child's parent and signing for my child.

❏   I am/am not receiving payment.

❏   I understand this material will not be used for any other purpose.

_____   _____
Signature   Date

_____   _____
Address   Phone number

_____   _____
Witness signature   Date

Use one form for each person.

:30 Second Script / Title _____ **Date** _____

1)

2)

3)

4)

5)

6)

7)

8)

Special instructions: _____

_____

_____

_____

_____

_____

_____

:60 Second Script / Title _____ **Date** _____

1)

2)

3)

4)

5)

6)

7)

8)

9)

10)

11)

12)

13)

14)

15)

16)

Special instructions: _____

_____

_____

Worksheet #1

Radio

HAVE YOUR REP FILL OUT AND RETURN THIS SHEET.

Radio Station Information

Call Letters _____   Dial Position _____

Rep's Name: _____   Phone Number: _____

Format: _____   Fax Number: _____

Demographic Strength: Sales Rep: Circle the choices from Groups A and B that best describe your station's primary strength.

Group A (age)	Group B (sex)
18–34	Female
18–49	Male
25–54	Adults (both male and female)
50+	

Cost per week based on frequency of 12X, 18X, 24X Monday – Friday 5:30A – 10 P.

12X per week	$ _____	(3X 5:30a – 10a, 3X 10a – 3p, 3X 3p –7p, 3X 7p – 10p)
18X per week	$ _____	(4X 5:30a – 10a, 5X 10a – 3p, 5X 3p –7p, 4X 7p – 10p)
24X per week	$ _____	(6X 5:30a – 10a, 6X 10a – 3p, 6X 3p –7p, 6X 7p – 10p)

Cost per week based on weekends (Friday –Sunday) 10A –10P.

12X per week	$ _____	(4X 10a – 3p, 4X 3p –7p, 4X 7p – 10p)
18X per week	$ _____	(6X 10a – 3p, 6X 3p –7p, 6X 7p – 10p)
24X per week	$ _____	(8X 10a – 3p, 8X 3p –7p, 8X 7p – 10p)

SPONSORSHIP AVAILABLE

Type of Sponsorship	Times per Week	Price per Week	Audience
News	2X (T, Th)	$ _____	_____ (age)
Billboards	3X (M, W, F)	$ _____	
are/are not included	5X (M – F)	$ _____	_____ (sex)
Weather	2X (T, Th)	$ _____	_____ (age)
Billboards	3X (M, W, F)	$ _____	
are/are not included	5X (M – F)	$ _____	_____ (sex)
Sports	2X (T, Th)	$ _____	_____ (age)
Billboards	3X (M, W, F)	$ _____	
are/are not included	5X (M – F)	$ _____	_____ (sex)
Air Traffic	2X (T, Th)	$ _____	_____ (age)
Billboards	3X (M, W, F)	$ _____	
are/are not included	5X (M – F)	$ _____	_____ (sex)

Worksheet #2

Radio

X = One Commercial

Station: _____

Sample General Weekday Schedules

12X	M	T	W	Th	F
6–10A	X		X		X
10–3P		X	X	X	
3–7P	X		X		X
7–10P		X	X	X	

Cost $ _____

18X	M	T	W	Th	F
6–10A	X		X	X	X
10–3P	X	X	X	X	X
3–7P	X	X	X	X	X
7–10P	X	X	X	X	

Cost $ _____

24X	M	T	W	Th	F
6–10A	XX	X	X	X	X
10–3P	X	X	XX	X	X
3–7P	X	XX	X	X	X
7–10P	X	X	X	XX	X

Cost $ _____

Sample Schedules for Early Mid-Week Business

12X	M	T	W
6–10A	X	X	X
10–3P	XX	X	X
3–7P	X	XX	
7–10P	X	X	

Cost $ _____

18X	M	T	W
6–10A	XX	X	XX
10–3P	XX	XX	XX
3–7P	XX	X	
7–10P	XX	XX	

Cost $ _____

24X	M	T	W
6–10A	XXX	XX	XX
10–3P	XX	XXX	XX
3–7P	XXX	XX	
7–10P	XX	XXX	

Cost $ _____

Sample Schedules for Late Week and Weekend Business

12X	M	T	W	Th	F	Sat
6–10A			X	X	X	
10–3P			X	X	X	
3–7P			X	X	X	
7–10P			X	X	X	

Cost $ _____

18X	M	T	W	Th	F	Sat
6–10A				X	X	XX
10–3P			XX	X	XX	
3–7P			X	XX	XX	
7–10P			X	XX	X	

Cost $ _____

24X	M	T	W	Th	F	Sat
6–10A			X	XX	XX	X
10–3P			X	X	XX	XX
3–7P			X	XX	XX	X
7–10P			X	XX	XX	X

Cost $ _____

Sample Schedules for Weekend Business

12X	F	Sat	Sun
6–10A			
10–3P		XX	XX
3–7P	XX	XX	
7–10P	XX	XX	

Cost $ _____

18X	F	Sat	Sun
6–10A			
10–3P		XXX	XXX
3–7P	XXX	XXX	
7–10P	XXX	XXX	

Cost $ _____

24X	F	Sat	Sun
6–10A			
10–3P		XXXX	XXXX
3–7P	XXXX	XXXX	
7–10P	XXXX	XXXX	

Cost $ _____

If you are not open Sunday or your event ends on Saturday, move Sunday spots back into Friday and Saturday.

Worksheet #3
Radio Demographic Rankings

Station: _____   Date: _____

Circle the same choices below from Groups A and B as you did in Chapter 1. Have your radio rep(s) fill out only the sections that match those selections. This worksheet, when completed by your reps, will indicate how the top four stations reaching your desired audience(s) compare to each other. The information will be excerpted from research companies such as Arbitron and Neilsen and represents the most accurate data available.

Group A (age)	Group B (sex)
18–34	Female
18–49	Male
25–54	Adults (both male and female)
50+	

Source: _____   Note to Rep: Please use average persons (00)
Market: Total Survey Area

Monday – Friday 5:30 AM to 10 PM

Women 18–34	Men 18–34	Adults 18–34
1. _____	_____	_____
2. _____	_____	_____
3. _____	_____	_____
4. _____	_____	_____

Women 18–49	Men 18–49	Adults 18–49
1. _____	_____	_____
2. _____	_____	_____
3. _____	_____	_____
4. _____	_____	_____

Women 25–54	Men 25–54	Adults 25–54
1. _____	_____	_____
2. _____	_____	_____
3. _____	_____	_____
4. _____	_____	_____

Women 50+	Men 50+	Adults 50+
1. _____	_____	_____
2. _____	_____	_____
3. _____	_____	_____
4. _____	_____	_____

Worksheet #3 # Radio Demographic Rankings, continued

Saturday – Sunday 9 AM to Midnight

Women 18–34	Men 18–34	Adults 18–34
1.		
2.		
3.		
4.		

Women 18–49	Men 18–49	Adults 18–49
1.		
2.		
3.		
4.		

Women 25–54	Men 25–54	Adults 25–54
1.		
2.		
3.		
4.		

Women 50+	Men 50+	Adults 50+
1.		
2.		
3.		
4.		

Notes: _____

_____

_____

_____

_____

_____

Submitted by: _____ _____ _____

　　　　　Name of Salesperson　　Station　　Date

Television Worksheet

HAVE YOUR REP FILL OUT AND RETURN THIS SHEET.

Note to Rep: Include only programs geared to the demographics indicated below.

Station _____   Dial Position _____

Rep's Name: _____   Phone: _____ Fax: _____

Owner: Circle choices from Groups A and B that correspond with page 4.

Group A (age)	Group B (sex)
18–34	Female
18–49	Male
25–54	Adults (both male and female)
50+	

Weekdays

Time Period	Program	Price per :30	Price per :10
_____	_____	$_____	$_____
_____	_____	$_____	$_____
_____	_____	$_____	$_____
_____	_____	$_____	$_____
_____	_____	$_____	$_____
_____	_____	$_____	$_____
_____	_____	$_____	$_____

Weekends

Time Period	Program	Price per :30	Price per :10
_____	_____	$_____	$_____
_____	_____	$_____	$_____
_____	_____	$_____	$_____
_____	_____	$_____	$_____
_____	_____	$_____	$_____
_____	_____	$_____	$_____
_____	_____	$_____	$_____

Print Worksheet

HAVE YOUR REP FILL OUT AND RETURN THIS SHEET.

Publication _____   Phone Number: _____

Rep's Name: _____   Fax Number: _____

☐ Daily   ☐ Weekly   ☐ Other

Ad Size	Price	Day Ad Would Run
Full Page	$_____	_____
1/2 Page	$_____	_____
1/4 Page	$_____	_____
1/8 Page	$_____	_____
Other	$_____	_____

Deadline for copy   _____

Cost of adding one color   _____

Special Sections Geared to this Business

Summer	Fall	Winter	Spring
_____	_____	_____	_____
_____	_____	_____	_____
_____	_____	_____	_____
_____	_____	_____	_____
_____	_____	_____	_____
_____	_____	_____	_____
_____	_____	_____	_____
_____	_____	_____	_____
_____	_____	_____	_____

Contract rate per column inch: $_____

Contract start date: _____   End date: _____

Direct Mail Worksheet

Company Name:_____   Sales Rep: _____

Address: _____   Phone Number: _____

_____   Fax: _____

❏ Mailings   ❏ Inserts

If inserts, name of publication: _____   Publication date: _____

Insertion cost per thousand: _____

Postage cost if mailing: _____   Mailing date: _____

Zip codes/areas covered: _____

Number of pieces: _____   Size of pieces: _____

How many colors/what specific colors: _____

Deadline for final design and copy: _____

Date of proof: _____   Changes made: _____

_____

_____

_____

Final approval date: _____

Total cost (including postage or insertion charge, tax, etc.) $ _____

Details of this direct mail campaign:_____

Offer or sale: _____

End date on offer: _____

Outdoor Billboard Worksheet

Company Name: _____   Rep's Name: _____

Phone Number: _____   Fax Number: _____

Board Size	Paint/Paper/Vinyl	Location	Monthly Rent	Date Available
_____	_____	_____	$ _____	_____
_____	_____	_____	$ _____	_____
_____	_____	_____	$ _____	_____
_____	_____	_____	$ _____	_____
_____	_____	_____	$ _____	_____
_____	_____	_____	$ _____	_____

Production cost: $ _____ every # _____ days. Contract dates: _____ to _____

Does contract have an automatic renewal clause?   Yes _____   No _____

Date of notification due: _____   In writing: Yes _____   No _____

Co-op being used?   Yes _____   No _____   What brand? _____

Special Instructions: _____

_____

_____

Sample Art Work

Multiple Boards

Board Number	Location	Up date	Down date	Production $	Monthly rent
_____	_____	_____	_____	_____	_____
_____	_____	_____	_____	_____	_____
_____	_____	_____	_____	_____	_____
_____	_____	_____	_____	_____	_____
_____	_____	_____	_____	_____	_____
_____	_____	_____	_____	_____	_____
_____	_____	_____	_____	_____	_____
_____	_____	_____	_____	_____	_____
_____	_____	_____	_____	_____	_____
_____	_____	_____	_____	_____	_____
_____	_____	_____	_____	_____	_____
_____	_____	_____	_____	_____	_____
_____	_____	_____	_____	_____	_____
_____	_____	_____	_____	_____	_____
_____	_____	_____	_____	_____	_____
_____	_____	_____	_____	_____	_____
_____	_____	_____	_____	_____	_____
_____	_____	_____	_____	_____	_____
_____	_____	_____	_____	_____	_____
_____	_____	_____	_____	_____	_____
_____	_____	_____	_____	_____	_____
_____	_____	_____	_____	_____	_____
_____	_____	_____	_____	_____	_____
_____	_____	_____	_____	_____	_____
_____	_____	_____	_____	_____	_____

Transit Worksheet #1

**Have your transit rep fill out this worksheet for your general information.
Use Worksheet #2 when you are actually ready to use this form of advertising.**

Company Name:_____   Phone Number: _____

Account Executive: _____   Fax Number: _____

Monthly Rent Per Bus

King size: $_____   Queen size: $ _____   Traveling Displays: $_____

Headlight signs: $ _____   Tail signs: $ _____   Driver signs: $_____

Bus wraps: $_____   Discounts available: _____

Production Cost

King size: $_____   Queen size: $ _____   Traveling Displays: $_____

Headlight signs: $ _____   Tail signs: $ _____   Driver signs: $_____

Bus wraps: $_____   Discounts available: _____

Side panel signs

King – 30" x 144"	Queen – 30" x 88"

Headlight signs

21" x 40"

Tail signs (top and bottom)

21" x 70"

Traveling display signs

21" x 44"

Interior signs

11" x 28"

Behind driver signs

14" x 19"

Transit Worksheet #2

Have your transit rep complete this worksheet when you are ready to advertise.

Company Name:_____ Phone Number: _____

Account Executive: _____ Fax Number: _____

Dates to schedule: _____ to _____ Number of weeks: _____

Total number of exterior signs: _____ Total number of interior signs: _____

# of King size: _____ # of Queen size:_____ # of Traveling Displays: _____

# of Headlight signs: _____ # of Tail signs:_____ # of Driver signs: _____

Campaign title:_____ Discount: _____

Production cost:$ _____ Rent per month:$_____ Total contract cost:$ _____

Specific routes: _____

_____

❑   Please check here to request rotation of bus(s) through all available routes.

Side panel signs

King – 30" x 144"   Queen – 30" x 88"

Headlight signs

21" x 40"

Tail signs (top and bottom)

21" x 70"

Traveling display signs

21" x 44"

Interior signs

11" x 28"

Behind driver signs

14" x 19"

Tracking Results Worksheet

Dates of campaign: _____ to _____ Total budget $ _____

Media used: ❏ Radio ❏ Television ❏ Print ❏ Direct Mail ❏ Outdoor

Radio stations and number of spots on each: _____

_____ Production/talent cost: $ _____

Length of radio spots ❏ 60 second spots ❏ 30 second spots

Total cost of radio: $ _____

Television stations and number of spots on each: _____

_____ Production/talent cost: $ _____

Length of television spots ❏ 10 second spots ❏ 30 second spots ❏ 60 second spots

Total cost of television: $ _____

Print/Publication(s) used: _____

Date of publication:_____ Second date: _____

Size of ad: _____ Size of second ad: _____

Total cost of print: $ _____

Number of direct mail pieces: _____

❏ Mailed

Date mailed: _____ Second mailing: _____

❏ Inserts

Publication used:_____

Date: _____ Second date: _____

Total cost of direct mail: $ _____

Outdoor billboards/company name: _____

Number of boards:_____ Size of boards: _____

Location of boards: _____

Total cost of outdoor: $ _____

The campaign had:❏ No results ❏ Some results ❏ Good results ❏ Great results

Notes: _____

_____

**Attach copies of radio and television scripts, print ads, and coupons to this sheet for future reference

Annual Tracking Worksheet

Year: _____ to _____ Total budget $ _____

Media used: ☐ Radio ☐ Television ☐ Print ☐ Direct Mail ☐ Outdoor ☐ Transit

Radio: Station/Total Amount/Discount %   **Television:** Station/Total Amount/Discount %

_____   _____

_____   _____

_____   _____

_____   _____

Radio Grand Total: $_____   **Television Grand Total: $** _____

Print: Publication   Daily/Weekly   Discount %   Total Amount

_____

_____

_____

_____

Print Grand Total: $ _____

Outdoor Billboards: Total Amount   **Direct Mail:**   Type   Total Amount
                        (rent and production)   (coupons, brochures, etc.)

_____   _____

_____   _____

_____   _____

_____   _____

Outdoor Grand Total: $ _____   **Direct Mail Grand Total: $** _____

Transit: Total Amount   Total # of Signs (exterior + interior)   Total # of Wraps

_____

_____

_____

_____

Transit Grand Total: $ _____

Co-op: _____ **Brands Used:** _____ **Total Amount:** _____

_____

_____

_____

Total Co-op Dollars Captured: $ _____

Index

From The Leading Publisher of Small Business Information
Books that save you time and money.

If you've ever wondered how to combine business success and personal significance, author Gerald Baron has some practical suggestions. After years of working with executives and entrepreneurs, he's found that business success and personal meaning can share a common ground. Using dozens of real-world examples, he shows hwo building relationships is the key to business development and personal fulfillment.

Friendship Marketing   **Pages: 183**
Paperback: $18.95   **ISBN: 1-55571-399-8**

The heart of customer service — the transaction between customer and service provider — is the focus of this book. Author Richard Gallagher demonstrates how the three secrets of customer service make these transactions satisfying and productive. An excellent follow-up to Stan Lindsay's *The Twenty-One Sales in a Sale*!

Smile Training Isn't Enough   **Pages: 200**
Paperback: $19.95   **ISBN: 1-55571-422-6**

With his expert advice and insight, author Jay Tolman goes beyond ordinary marketing and advertising books to provide a variety of strategies for your marketing needs. He focuses not on prescribing the "best" marketing method, but on using a combination of dozens of marketing techniques, teaching readers to evaluate many marketing angles. Being capable of this will only better prepare you for the challenges of marketing in the years to come.

Marketing for the New Millenium   **Pages: 200**
Paperback: $18.95   **ISBN: 1-55571-432-3**

As marketing goes increasingly global, CEOs and sales-and-marketing execs are scrambling to keep up — to position their products correctly in the international marketplace, or just to begin exploring sales avenues outside of the United States. *Developing International Markets* is ideal for anyone interested in this arena. It provides information on what to expect, how to avoid fruitless marketing activities, how to find local marketing agents, plus it covers the requirements that are often overlooked.

Developing International Markets   **Pages: 340**
Paperback: $19.95   **ISBN: 1-55571-433-1**

The Oasis Press® Order Form

WAG07/98

Call, Mail, Email, or Fax Your Order to: PSI Research, P.O. Box 3727, Central Point, OR 97502
Email: sales@psi-research.com   Website: http://www.psi-research.com
Order Phone USA & Canada: +1 800 228-2275   Inquiries & International Orders: +1 541 479-9464   Fax: +1 541 476-1479

TITLE	✔ BINDER	✔ PAPERBACK	QUANTITY	COST
Advertising Without An Agency		❑ $19.95		
Bottom Line Basics	❑ $39.95	❑ $19.95		
BusinessBasics: A Microbusiness Startup Guide		❑ $17.95		
The Business Environmental Handbook	❑ $39.95	❑ $19.95		
Business Owner's Guide to Accounting & Bookkeeping		❑ $19.95		
Buyer's Guide to Business Insurance	❑ $39.95	❑ $19.95		
California Corporation Formation Package	❑ $39.95	❑ $29.95		
Collection Techniques for a Small Business	❑ $39.95	❑ $19.95		
A Company Policy and Personnel Workbook	❑ $49.95	❑ $29.95		
Company Relocation Handbook	❑ $39.95	❑ $19.95		
CompControl: The Secrets of Reducing Worker's Compensation Costs	❑ $39.95	❑ $19.95		
Complete Book of Business Forms		❑ $19.95		
Connecting Online: Creating a Successful Image on the Internet		❑ $21.95		
Customer Engineering: Cutting Edge Selling Strategies	❑ $39.95	❑ $19.95		
Develop & Market Your Creative Ideas		❑ $15.95		
Developing International Markets		❑ $19.95		
Doing Business in Russia		❑ $19.95		
Draw The Line: A Sexual Harassment Free Workplace		❑ $17.95		
Entrepreneurial Decisionmaking		❑ $19.95		
The Essential Corporation Handbook		❑ $21.95		
The Essential Limited Liability Company Handbook	❑ $39.95	❑ $21.95		
Export Now: A Guide for Small Business	❑ $39.95	❑ $24.95		
Financial Decisionmaking: A Guide for the Non-Accountant		❑ $19.95		
Financial Management Techniques for Small Business	❑ $39.95	❑ $19.95		
Financing Your Small Business		❑ $19.95		
Franchise Bible: How to Buy a Franchise or Franchise Your Own Business	❑ $39.95	❑ $24.95		
Friendship Marketing: Growing Your Business by Cultivating Strategic Relationships		❑ $18.95		
Funding High-Tech Ventures		❑ $21.95		
Home Business Made Easy		❑ $19.95		
Information Breakthrough		❑ $22.95		
The Insider's Guide to Small Business Loans	❑ $29.95	❑ $19.95		
InstaCorp – Incorporate In Any State (Book & Software)		❑ $29.95		
Joysticks, Blinking Lights and Thrills		❑ $18.95		
Keeping Score: An Inside Look at Sports Marketing		❑ $18.95		
Know Your Market: How to Do Low-Cost Market Research	❑ $39.95	❑ $19.95		
The Leader's Guide		❑ $19.95		
Legal Expense Defense: How to Control Your Business' Legal Costs and Problems	❑ $39.95	❑ $19.95		
Location, Location, Location: How to Select the Best Site for Your Business		❑ $19.95		
Mail Order Legal Guide	❑ $45.00	❑ $29.95		
Managing People: A Practical Guide		❑ $21.95		
Marketing for the New Millennium: Applying New Techniques		❑ $19.95		
Marketing Mastery: Your Seven Step Guide to Success	❑ $39.95	❑ $19.95		
The Money Connection: Where and How to Apply for Business Loans and Venture Capital	❑ $39.95	❑ $24.95		
Moonlighting: Earn a Second Income at Home		❑ $15.95		
People Investment	❑ $39.95	❑ $19.95		
Power Marketing for Small Business	❑ $39.95	❑ $19.95		
Profit Power: 101 Pointers to Give Your Business a Competitive Edge		❑ $19.95		
Proposal Development: How to Respond and Win the Bid	❑ $39.95	❑ $21.95		
Raising Capital		❑ $19.95		
Renaissance 2000: Liberal Arts Essentials for Tomorrow's Leaders		❑ $22.95		
Retail in Detail: How to Start and Manage a Small Retail Business		❑ $15.95		
Secrets to High Ticket Selling		❑ $19.95		
Secrets to Buying and Selling a Business		❑ $24.95		
Secure Your Future: Financial Planning at Any Age	❑ $39.95	❑ $19.95		
The Small Business Insider's Guide to Bankers		❑ $18.95		
SmartStart Your (State) Business... series		❑ $19.95		
PLEASE SPECIFY WHICH STATE(S) YOU WANT:				
Smile Training Isn't Enough: The Three Secrets to Excellent Customer Service		❑ $19.95		
Start Your Business (Available as a book and disk package)		❑ $ 9.95 (without disk)		

BOOK SUB-TOTAL (Additional titles on other side)

TITLE	✔ BINDER	✔ PAPERBACK	QUANTITY	COST
Starting and Operating a Business in...series *Includes FEDERAL section PLUS ONE STATE section*	❑ $34.95	❑ $27.95		
PLEASE SPECIFY WHICH STATE(S) YOU WANT:				
STATE SECTION ONLY (BINDER NOT INCLUDED) SPECIFY STATE(S):	❑ $8.95			
FEDERAL SECTION ONLY (BINDER NOT INCLUDED)	❑ $12.95			
U.S. EDITION (FEDERAL SECTION – 50 STATES AND WASHINGTON DC IN 11-BINDER SET)	❑ $295.95			
Successful Business Plan: Secrets & Strategies	❑ $49.95	❑ $27.95		
Successful Network Marketing for The 21st Century		❑ $15.95		
Surviving Success		❑ $19.95		
TargetSmart! Database Marketing for the Small Business		❑ $19.95		
Top Tax Saving Ideas for Today's Small Business		❑ $16.95		
Twenty-One Sales in a Sale: What Sales Are You Missing?		❑ $19.95		
Which Business? Help in Selecting Your New Venture		❑ $18.95		
Write Your Own Business Contracts	❑ $39.95	❑ $24.95		
BOOK SUB-TOTAL (Be sure to figure your amount from the previous side)				

OASIS SOFTWARE   Please specify which computer operating system you use (DOS, MacOS, or Windows)

TITLE	✔ Windows	✔ MacOS	Price	QUANTITY	COST
California Corporation Formation Package ASCII Software	❑	❑	$ 39.95		
Company Policy & Personnel Software Text Files	❑	❑	$ 49.95		
Financial Management Techniques (Full Standalone)	❑		$ 99.95		
Financial Templates	❑	❑	$ 69.95		
The Insurance Assistant Software (Full Standalone)	❑		$ 29.95		
Start Your Business (Software for Windows™)	❑		$ 19.95		
Successful Business Plan (Software for Windows™)	❑		$ 99.95		
Successful Business Plan Templates	❑	❑	$ 69.95		
The Survey Genie - Customer Edition (Full Standalone)	❑ $199.95 (WIN)	❑ $149.95 (DOS)			
The Survey Genie - Employee Edition (Full Standalone)	❑ $199.95 (WIN)	❑ $149.95 (DOS)			
SOFTWARE SUB-TOTAL					

BOOK & DISK PACKAGES   Please specify which computer operating system you use (DOS, MacOS, or Windows)

TITLE	✔ Windows	✔ MacOS	✔ Binder	✔ Paperback	QUANTITY	COST
The Buyer's Guide to Business Insurance w/ Insurance Assistant	❑		❑ $ 59.95	❑ $ 39.95		
California Corporation Formation Binder Book & ASCII Software	❑	❑	❑ $ 69.95	❑ $ 59.95		
Company Policy & Personnel Book & Software Text Files	❑	❑	❑ $ 89.95	❑ $ 69.95		
Financial Management Techniques Book & Software	❑		❑ $129.95	❑ $ 119.95		
Start Your Business Paperback & Software (Software for Windows™)	❑			❑ $ 24.95		
Successful Business Plan Book & Software for Windows™	❑		❑ $125.95	❑ $109.95		
Successful Business Plan Book & Software Templates	❑	❑	❑ $109.95	❑ $ 89.95		
BOOK & DISK PACKAGE SUB-TOTAL						

AUDIO CASSETTES

	✔ PAPERBACK	QUANTITY	COST
Power Marketing Tools For Small Business	❑ $ 49.95		
The Secrets To Buying & Selling A Business	❑ $ 49.95		
AUDIO CASSETTES SUB-TOTAL			

Sold To: **Please give street address**

NAME: _____

Title: _____

Company: _____

Street Address: _____

City/State/Zip: _____

Daytime Phone: _____ Email: _____

Ship To: **If different than above, please give alternate street address**

NAME: _____

Title: _____

Company: _____

Street Address: _____

City/State/Zip: _____

Daytime Phone: _____

Your Grand Total

SUB-TOTALS (from other side) $ _____

SUB-TOTALS (from this side) $ _____

SHIPPING (see chart below) $ _____

TOTAL ORDER $ _____

If your purchase is:	Shipping costs within the USA:
$0 - $25	$5.00
$25.01 - $50	$6.00
$50.01 - $100	$7.00
$100.01 - $175	$9.00
$175.01 - $250	$13.00
$250.01 - $500	$18.00
$500.01+	4% of total merchandise

07/98

Payment Information: **Rush service is available, call for details.**
International and Canadian Orders: Please call for quote on shipping.

❑ CHECK Enclosed payable to PSI Research   Charge: ❑ VISA   ❑ MASTERCARD   ❑ AMEX   ❑ DISCOVER

Card Number: _____ Expires: _____

Signature: _____ Name On Card: _____